BY THE SAME AUTHOR

The Brotherhood of Angels and of Men
Be Ye Perfect
The Angelic Hosts
Fairies at Work and at Play
The Kingdom of Faerie
Health and the Spiritual Life
New Light on the Problem of Disease
An Occult View of Health and Disease
First Steps on the Path
Thus Have I Heard
The Inner Side of Church Worship
The Science of Seership
Clairvoyance and the Serpent Fire
The Coming of the Angels
Some Experiments in Four-Dimensional Vision
Destiny
The Miracle of Birth
Meditations on the Occult Life
Reincarnation: Fact or Fallacy?
The Seven Human Temperaments
The Kingdom of the Gods
Theosophy Answers Some Problems of Life
Through the Gateway of Death
The Pathway to Perfection
Occult Powers in Nature and in Man
The School of the Wisdom Lecture Notes, Vols. I & II.
Man's Supersensory and Spiritual Powers
Authentic Stories of Intelligence in Animals
An Animals' Bill of Rights

VITAL QUESTIONS ANSWERED

BY

GEOFFREY HODSON

PRINTED IN INDIA

At the Vasanta Press, The Theosophical Society,
Adyar, Madras 20.

INTRODUCTION

During the last few years Mr. Geoffrey Hodson has given many Public Lectures from the platform of the H.P.B. Lodge of the Theosophical Society in Auckland, New Zealand. At the conclusion of each Address written questions were invited from members of the audience. These questions often covered a wide range of subjects, many relating to matters quite outside the scope of the lecture.

As Chairman at many of these Meetings, I was able to appreciate better than most Mr. Hodson's ability to deal with his listeners' problems in a helpful and sympathetic manner. His answers revealed his deep knowledge of Theosophy and many related subjects. They also showed an amazing grasp of detail and the ability to conjure up at a moment's notice the right phrase, an appropriate passage from one of the Sacred Scriptures of the world, or some apt quotation or illustration from theosophical sources. Some of these questions and answers were taken down in shorthand and have been gathered together in this Volume.

As one observes Mr. Hodson carrying out this part of his programme at Public Lectures, one can hardly fail to be struck by his evident wish to penetrate to the heart of the queries and to meet as fully as possible the questioners' needs for further information. He takes the utmost care with every question, however simple and even unnecessary it may appear, always finding something interesting and helpful to say, whether the enquiry concerns personal problems of health and happiness—which he often seems to perceive intuitively—or philosophic and occult knowledge.

The question and answer method of presenting Theosophy has been used before, notably by Madame Blavatsky in *The Key to Theosophy* and by P. Pavri in *Theosophy Explained*, but these writers wrote both question and reply. It should be remembered that Mr. Hodson did not enjoy this advantage and that he had only a few seconds to study each question before replying.

Now that these questions and answers are being published, I am sure readers all over the world will find them as helpful and interesting as we did in Auckland when we first heard them.

MILTON THORNTON
President,
H. P. B. Lodge, Auckland,
New Zealand
1951-54

AUTHOR'S PREFACE

THEOSOPHY, being Divine Wisdom, is necessarily abstract and infinite. Although man's power of comprehension continually increases—naturally as a result of evolution and enforcedly as a result of regular study, meditation and a spiritual mode of life—his finite mind can never wholly grasp that which is infinite, and a complete exposition of any theosophical subject is not humanly possible. In consequence, no exponent of Theosophy below the rank of an Adept—and such a one would hardly be likely to do so—can legitimately make either authoritative or complete pronouncements concerning its teachings; he can only put forward his own necessarily limited opinions. My answers to questions sent up by members of Auckland audiences can in no way be regarded as complete expositions of the subjects with which they deal. Brevity and the more immediate mental satisfaction of questioners were regarded as being of first importance when making my replies.

The questions put to me by members of the public chiefly concern theosophical doctrines, philosophic and religious ideas, the results of occult investigations and, in some cases, objective facts. Answers to such questions must therefore be adapted as closely as possible to the levels of thought and enquiry from which they are put—more generally that of the formal, analytical mind. Nevertheless, even while answering certain types of questions, I realise that very often the questioners could, and ideally should, answer them for themselves. To achieve this, however, a certain intensity of purpose, a determination to discover truth direct, and the employment of an effective technique of inducing mental sensitivity and stilling the mind, are necessary. Then a student may become illumined by his own spiritually intuited knowledge, which is far more valuable than information received without due mental effort and from an external source.

I have even thought that such answering of questions, from one point of view, might almost be harmful. When intellectually satisfying, an answer could possibly bring further research to an end, tend to put the minds of enquirers to sleep. Puzzles, apparent paradoxes, perplexities and apparent contradictions should, on the contrary, serve as spurs, stimulating the student to embark upon the interior search for truth. This applies especially to ideas which have within them those deeply mystical elements which almost evade, particularly at first, purely rational comprehension and exposition. Even whilst recognising this, I always heartily welcome the questions put to me by members of my audiences, being only too thankful that they attend my lectures and are genuinely seeking for truth. Many of them may be hearing of Theosophy for the first time and therefore could not be expected to embark at once upon an interior search for knowledge. Ideally, I presume, theosophical lecturers and class leaders should answer questions in such a way that the immediate demand for an explanation is met and enquirers are *also* encouraged to continue their own researches. A teacher was once asked why God does not always answer our prayers. He replied: "Perhaps because we would then stop praying."

If readers, particularly well-instructed Theosophists, should conclude that the way in which the answers recorded in this book were couched could tend to make them too final, and so appear to close the subject, it should be remembered that a fairly full exposition had preceded and evoked the questions. Furthermore, the time available after a lecture is always short, and I regard it as most important that no one who comes to a theosophical Meeting in search of information and help should be either repelled or unsatisfied. Both the lecture itself and the answers to questions should at least demonstrate that the teachings of Theosophy provide a reasonable explanation of the mysteries of life and helpful solutions of human problems, international, national and personal.

In this book of collected questions and extempore answers the informal, conversational style in which the answers were given has been largely preserved. Apart from changes of construction necessary to make the meaning clearer, no attempt at complete literary perfection has been made. Quotations have been checked and their references provided. Occasionally additional information and comments on later world events have been added to the original answers, partly by means of footnotes. In the main, however, they are here presented very much as they were given at the time. The titles of each of the Nine Parts of the book and of their component Chapters indicate the subject-matter of the lectures which evoked the questions.

GEOFFREY HODSON

Auckland, New Zealand
1955

CONTENTS

PART FOUR

ADEPTSHIP AND THE ADEPTS

PART FIVE

THE SPIRITUAL LIFE

PART SIX

THE SACRED LANGUAGE OF ALLEGORY AND SYMBOL

PART SEVEN

THEOSOPHICAL ANSWERS TO HUMAN PROBLEMS

PART EIGHT
MAN'S SUPERSENSORY POWERS

PART NINE
HEALTH AND DISEASE

PART ONE

INDIVIDUAL AND RACIAL EVOLUTION

1. Early Races of Man

Question: How did the first two Root Races[1] spend their lives? What were their occupations?

Answer: I do not suppose it is within our capacity to conceive of their occupations. They were living in the etheric and superphysical worlds, with all the resultant freedom of movement and wide expanse or range of planetary aura in which to move. The astral plane of the planet reaches nearly to the Moon, so that presumably there would have been all that superphysical area open to them. There would also have been the various sub-planes and their phenomena, of which there is nothing comparable in physical life that I can

[1] Root Races. According to theosophical ethnology, seven basic human types called Root Races occupy a planet in succession. Lemuria and Atlantis are names given to continents now submerged beneath the Pacific and Atlantic Oceans respectively. They were the homes of the third and fourth of the seven major Races of men to occupy this planet. The present Aryan Race and language group is the fifth of these. The first two Races, being on the downward arc, wore superphysical and etheric bodies only. *Vide The Solar System*, A. E. Powell, T.P.H., London.

think of. They would have been aware of each other—the first Race chiefly through a form of the sense of hearing, and the second Race with the added sense of touch. There would also have been some telepathic interchange going on between them.

No sense of separateness as we know it caused them to make errors, so there would have been no severe adversities of *karma*.[1] Their lives would have been perfectly happy and their bodies not subject to mortality or disease.

From our point of view they would have been rather sleepy, being somewhat in the larval stage, with variations in degree of awareness according to individual development. Occupation, in the sense of doing something or having duties, would not exist. All was concentrated in being, in existence, in emotional states—especially the sense of touch. They might, probably would, have been able to see psychically, and perhaps sense, the physical Earth —particularly its astral and its etheric double—and would doubtless have been partially aware of the cataclysmic life of the planet as it gradually cooled

[1] *Karma* (*Sk.*). The universal law of cause and effect, which guides unerringly all other laws productive of certain effects along the grooves of their respective causations. This law operates not only during a single life, but throughout successive lives, the conditions and opportunities of which are the exact effects of causes generated in preceding incarnations. Absolute justice is by this law assured to every human being. Cf. *Galatians*, VI:7.

from the radiantly hot stage down to a physically inhabitable condition.

They lived in association with the so-called Polar and Hyperborean continents, which stretched southward from the North Pole and included Greenland, Kamschatka and Scandinavia. Their superphysical and etheric bodies have been described as glowing with golden yellow and orange colours. These etheric men, who belonged to the second Root Race of men upon Earth, were almost tree-like in shape, but approaching animal and semi-human types in outline. They drifted, gliding amidst the brilliantly green tropical forests. They had no trace of sex and multiplied by expansion and budding, though later by extrusion of procreative germs, so that their progeny were called " sweat-born ".

Later, a vast primeval forest would also have provided a pleasant environment, amidst the astro-etheric double and emanations of which they would have floated and had some contact with the ensouling Life of the great trees.

2. Atlantis and the Atlanteans

Question: Will Atlantis ever rise again?

Answer: According to the findings and teachings of occult science, yes. After its soil has been rested and recuperated, Atlantis is to rise once more to be the home of a future Root Race. The continental home of the first Root Race was at the North Polar Cap. The second Race was called the Hyperborean, and occupied a continent which stretched from the North Pole southwards to include North Asia, Scandinavia, Greenland and Kamschatka. The third Race occupied Lemuria, on a remnant of which we here in New Zealand are now living; it stretched roughly from East Africa to Western South America, and included southerly portions of Asia and the Far East. Thus Lemuria was a vast continent, eventually being broken up by internal fires and volcanoes which caused the main body of land to sink beneath the waves of the Pacific Ocean. It also will rise again and be the home of a still later Race of men. After Lemuria came Atlantis and then our present continents. Parts of these will sink in their turn as the now engulfed land masses rise again.

Question: Are the Maoris Atlanteans in the main?

Answer: They may have some Atlantean blood, though there is said to be evidence that they are Aryan in origin, some ethnologists tracing their ancestry to Egypt and others to India. Their language, as well as their features, would strongly suggest that they have a close link with India. Many of their words—the suffix " manu " and the word " ariki ", for example—have Sanskrit roots and that is the language associated with the early Indo-Aryan peoples, being still spoken in some parts of India. Numbers of Maoris have the straight Aryan features and brown hair; thus it may be assumed that many of them are a mixture of Aryan, Atlantean, and some Polynesian and Melanesian Races. Their esoteric religion, or white *tohungism*, contains many tenets, practices, and even names, to be found in the religions of Aryan peoples.

Question: Why, since the help of the Adepts was received, did the Atlantean civilisation degenerate?

Answer: Just as a mother must eventually withdraw her sustaining hands from a child in order that it may learn how to walk and to balance and to develop strength to bear its own weight, even though it will fall in the process, so the great Guardians and Teachers of young humanity support it only just as long as is wise. They then begin *very gradually*, over a period of thousands of years, to withdraw from close physical intercourse with the Race, leaving it to learn to stand on its own feet. They continue, however, to inspire and to guide mentally and spiritually. At intervals there appears on Earth a great World Teacher such as Hermes, "The Thrice Greatest", who came to ancient Egypt, and the Lord Vyasa, the Lord Shri Krishna, the Lord Buddha and

Shri Shankaracharya, who came to India. The Lord Orpheus came to Greece and Zoroaster to the Persians, and these visitations by lofty Personages reached their culmination two thousand years ago in the appearance on Earth of the Second Aspect of the Blessed Trinity as the Lord of Love, the Lord Jesus Christ.

In these ways the Perfected Ones come personally and physically amongst us. They also send inspired Prophets, Seers and Initiated Disciples to help us. So They do not neglect us but, like the child, the Race must learn to stand alone, even though it disregards the guidance of its Elders and so has its falls.

The degeneration of the Atlantean peoples to which you refer occurred after the physical departure of the Adept Teachers, who were the Divine Dynasties of Kings to which the literature of ancient peoples refers. Happily, the spiritual guidance of mankind by Earth's Adepts still continues. The coming again of Theosophy to the world towards the end of the 19th century was a part of that guidance.

I repeat that this wonderful gift of the Ancient Wisdom should not be regarded as a set of dogmas but as a kind of wonderful sunlight to the mind, its beams penetrating the clouded intellect of man and lighting up both his mind and his life.

3. Human Life on Other Planets

Question: Can you name all ten planets? Has one, as legend says, exploded into the Asteroids? Where do these come in? Do any of them hold life? Why are only seven planets visible? What role does Vulcan fill?

Answer: I can name the planets of seven of our Planetary Schemes.[1] There are ten in all but three of them, I understand, have no physical planets at present and are therefore unnamed. The names and evolutionary positions of the seven Sacred Planets, as they are called in occult literature, are:

Vulcan, in its third Chain.
Venus, in its fifth Chain.
Earth, in its fourth Chain, which is said to include Mars and Mercury.
Jupiter, in its third Chain.
Saturn, in its third Chain.
Uranus, in its third Chain.
Neptune, in its fourth Chain.

These are the only seven planets of which we have had any theosophical information as being the physical planets of Planetary Schemes.

[1] Planetary Schemes. In occult science the Solar System is said to consist of ten Planetary Schemes, each composed of seven successive Chains of Globes, superphysical and physical. Each Chain is composed of seven Rounds, during each of which the Life-stream, bearing with it the evolving beings, travels once round the seven Globes. The period of occupation of one of the seven Globes is called a World Period. *Vide The Solar System*, A.E. Powell.

I have not found any theosophical statement confirming one astronomical view that the Asteroids are the result of an explosion of a planet. They will certainly contain life, for there is no such thing as dead matter. Even mineral substance is instinct with life. Every atom of every mineral, as well, of course, as of every plant, animal and human body, is charged to the full, almost to bursting point, with the wondrous Power, Life and Consciousness—the very Presence—of the Supreme Intelligence of our Solar System, sometimes called the Solar Logos.

Vast though theosophical information is in our day, we are informed that it is only a fragment of the totality of knowledge in the charge of the great Adept Keepers of the Sacred Light throughout the ages. In Their wisdom They preserved it against loss, particularly through the successive Dark Ages, and age by age They reveal parts of it which would be useful to humanity. Remember that that which we now have, which seems to us so great and wonderful, the Theosophy of our age, is only a fragment of the great totality of knowledge. Only a corner of the curtain has been lifted, as one of the great Teachers has said.

Question: How do we evolve from one planet to the next?

Answer: If you mean how do we move from one planet to its successor, Theosophy teaches that the life on each planet is in charge of a very mighty Intelligence, an Adept Member of the Solar Hierarchy of both Superhuman and Archangelic and angelic Officers and servants of the Supreme Will and Law. The life of a single Round, during which the Life-wave travels round the seven Globes of a Planetary Chain, is in charge of a very great Being called a Round Manu. He holds the Round within His consciousness and, through His subordinates, directs the whole process of involution and evolution that occurs in His Round. It is He, this very high Official, who absorbs into His aura all the seeds of Life and all the Monad-Egos of men at the end of a World Period, and conveys them through the superphysical worlds to the next Globe, Round or Chain at the end of an epoch. All these great processes are under the direction of high Officials, and the Solar Logos is in charge of the evolution of Life and form throughout the whole Solar System. One of the Seven Mighty Spirits before the Throne, also referred to as the Archangels of the Face, is in charge of one of the seven Planetary Schemes. Within each Scheme, Lords of Chains and Rounds preserve and transfer Life and consciousness from one Chain, Round or Globe to its successor.

This is hinted at in the Bible, if under an allegorical veil. In one meaning Noah and his

Ark is a symbol or glyph of a great Being who, at the end of a period—onset of the Flood—receives into His aura—His "ark"—the seeds of Life and living beings. There He preserves them during a period of quiescence—the Flood—and then transfers them to the next and higher system of manifestation—Mount Ararat, the dry land after the flood had receded, and the post-deluvian epoch.

Question: Is scientific knowledge, especially of electricity and atomic energy, more advanced on Mars than on Earth?

Answer: About atomic energy I know nothing, but the use of electricity to meet human needs is very advanced, it is said. (*Vide The Solar System*, A. E. Powell.)

Question: How far does the astral sphere of Mars spread (in miles)?

Answer: I understand that when Mars is at its nearest [1] to Earth, then the astral bodies of the two planets touch. I have been given to understand—

[1] The mean distance is about 48,292,400 miles. A calculation has been attempted on the following lines: The astral bodies of the Earth and the Moon have been said to overlap at their minimum distance apart, which is 221,463 miles. Since the Earth is about 4 times larger than the Moon, it seems reasonable to assume that the Earth's astral body will also be 4 times larger than that of the Moon. If this is true, then the radius of the Earth's astral body is 181,133 miles and its diameter 362,266 miles. The radius of the Moon's astral body is 45,322 miles and its diameter 90,644 miles. The same reasoning might possibly be applied to the planet Mars, which is 48,292,400 miles away from the Earth.

and this is merely offered as a student's thoughts—that at that time it is possible to cross to Mars and for Martians to cross over here in the astral body. There might be a danger, however, of getting stranded. When the planets begin to separate, the astral auras would also part. The mental bodies of the planets extend much further than the astral bodies, so that if you were able to function in your mental body you could leave your astral behind on the Earth and travel in your mental body. This process continues until, it is predicated, the centre of the Solar System on the higher plane can be reached. At that level there would be little or no necessity for travel, the whole Solar System being within the range of consciousness all at once. At the mental and astral levels, however, travel *would* be necessary to reach extra-terrestrial planets.

Question: Could the Martians contribute to our enlightenment on philosophic illumination?

Answer: That would depend upon the individual inhabitant of Mars. Most of the Martians are said to be concentrating upon the use of the formal, concrete mind, which tends to be severely analytical and factual. Such men would hardly be likely to have any greater grasp of philosophic principles than well-informed students of philosophy on our Earth.

PART TWO

SUCCESSIVE LIVES ON EARTH

1. Reincarnation

Question: Does belief in Theosophy include a belief in Reincarnation? [1]

Answer: No, definitely not. Belief in Theosophy does not necessarily include a belief in any particular doctrine. Theosophy is only a group of ideas offered for consideration. Students who discover the teachings think them out for themselves and accept, reject or suspend judgment as they feel moved. The theosophical student and member is not in a prison of any kind whatsoever. He has found complete freedom of thought and of its expression within the limits of brotherhood and courtesy. He may discover an idea, examine it, then reject or accept it, as the case may be. So it is with Reincarnation and all the other wonderful ideas included in the group of such doctrines known as Theosophy. My answer, therefore, is: " No,

[1] *Reincarnation*. The process of human evolution to perfection by means of successive lives on Earth under *kārmic* law.

Theosophy does not include belief in Reincarnation or, indeed, in anything else." I do think, however, that most Theosophists have thought their way through to a belief in Reincarnation. They have found that the twin doctrines of evolution to perfection by means of successive lives on Earth and the law of cause and effect make possible a logical solution to the difficult problems of human life, and particularly that of seeming injustice. *Vide Reincarnation—Fact or Fallacy?*, Geoffrey Hodson, T. P. H., Adyar, Madras, India.

Question: How many incarnations does one have per Planetary Cycle?

Answer: May I alter the question a little, to bring it within more easily comprehensible terms? How many human incarnations are normally required to reach Adeptship? Nowhere have I found a precise statement, but there are hints that the number seven governs the process and that between seven hundred and eight hundred lives may be needed. Remember, however, that we have the power to hasten our evolution and so reduce the number of lives required. In Buddhism it is taught that when once a person receives or experiences what the Lord Buddha called " the thought of enlightenment ", then their evolution is speeded up. When what we Christians would call true spiritual conversion or rebirth has once happened, then, it is said, the goal of perfected manhood can be reached in seven more lives.

Question: Are Reincarnation and Resurrection the same thing?

Answer: Not quite, especially in the accepted Christian view of a single bodily resurrection to occur on the Day of Judgment, or the last day. (*John* VI: 39). Such a doctrine is very difficult to believe, for the body will have disintegrated. Indeed, according to the doctrine of Reincarnation there will have been some seven hundred bodies and the question arises, in which of them will we be resurrected? Such a teaching of bodily resurrection bristles with difficulties. However, there is an occult significance contained within the idea of resurrection, namely the attainment of the power—which will one day come to all of us—to leave the body freely at will and without a break in consciousness, so that it is no longer as a closed tomb.

Even now there are people who can do that. Some of us have had the experience, have we not, of being free of the body and seeing it lying down while we are hovering near. That is the beginning of the resurrection attainment. One day we shall be able to leave the body at will, without a break in consciousness, to travel, investigate, explore the inner, higher worlds, come back with the fruits of our research, wake the body up and retain the full memory of what has taken place. That attainment is technically, in occult parlance, the Resurrection. The rolling away of the stone from the tomb of Our Lord is interpreted to mean the opening of the "stone" or *chakram* at the crown of the head, through which the Inner Self can depart and return at will. Reincarnation, on the other hand, implies evolution to perfected manhood by means of successive lives on Earth.

Question: Does the Ego reincarnate or the Monad?

Answer: You are here introducing technical terms which should first of all be explained to those who may this evening be attending our meetings for the first time.

In Theosophy man is described as being triple—the outer, personal, mortal man; the inner, reincarnating Spiritual Soul which we call the Ego; and the still higher, finer Self, the Spark of the Divine Flame, the Scintilla of the Spiritual Sun, the Dweller in the Innermost, called in philosophy the Monad or the One. Thus there exist the inner, highest spiritual consciousness, the Monad; the reincarnating Spiritual Soul of Will, Wisdom and Intelligence, and the outer, bodily man consisting of mind, emotion, vitality and flesh. Actually the Monad and the Ego cannot be regarded as separate, since the Ego is but a manifestation of a ray of the Monad. Therefore you find some writers using the term " Monad-Ego ". It is the Monad-Ego of man which is making the great pilgrimage to perfection and which is continually reborn. I must here add that Man-Spirit, or the Monad, is in no sense different or separate from God-Spirit, or the Monad of the universe. In one sense man has no separate, individually possessed portion of pure Spirit which belongs to him alone. His Spirit is but a ray of Universal Spirit, with which the Spiritual Selves of all men are equally interfused. This is, however, not merely a doctrine concerning man; it is also an experience to be entered into, a direct knowledge to be gained, an illumination which is within the reach of those who will seek it ardently and by the proper means. Cosmic consciousness is one name for this direct experience of the unity and the identity of the Spirit of man with the Spirit of the universe, man with God.

Question: Is it possible to demonstrate Reincarnation in the same way that Dr. J. B. Rhine is doing with thought transference?

Answer: No, I do not think so. Evidence of many kinds exists, but it is not final, demonstrable proof. There are people who, when describing a remembered past life, correctly relate historical events concerning which they could not otherwise have been aware. This is strong evidence—and there are many such cases—but it is not proof.

Accurate clairvoyance could reveal the same facts. The unusual powers of child geniuses and prodigies are only explained in terms of logic by the fact of the Ego having brought over from preceding lives an acquired and highly developed faculty. Instinct, antipathy and sympathy without obvious reason are also said to be the results of such memories, but they are not proofs.

I personally think that one of the strongest supporting evidences for rebirth is the existence of masculine types of women and feminine types of men, both being common phenomena. The masculine type of woman may have been a man in a previous life, still retaining the attributes, the impressions and the tendencies of masculinity. Similarly, feminine types of men were perhaps women in the past and possibly in more than one immediately preceding life. These again, however, are only evidences and not demonstrable proofs.

The only personal proof is one's own direct recollection or Egoic awareness of one's own past lives, just as one is aware of yesterday. Even then, as in all metaphysical and spiritual realisations, such experiences can only be true to one's own consciousness. They are proof to the illumined one, but that proof cannot be demonstrably conveyed to another. Words may describe such discovered truth, philosophers, poets and artists may portray it, but it is the inner experience alone which is final demonstration and proof of its truthfulness. So I must answer you: "No, I do not think that Reincarnation, or even the life after death, can be externally demonstrated beyond all possibility of doubt."

Though, at first thought, this may appear to be somewhat disheartening, there could, I suggest, be much value in the limitation; for it forces upon each sincere seeker for truth the necessity of finding his or her own light, of establishing themselves in a faith which, being founded upon direct, first-hand, interior experience, is unshakeable. This attainment of interior light, and perhaps still more the effort made in reaching it, are of the greatest possible value in the development of the human mind and intuitive faculty.

Question: Would you kindly say how many lives are spent in incarnation on this Earth?

Answer: Nowhere have I found that information exactly stated, but hints appear here and there in occult literature. It seems that the number seven has an influence in this matter, as in so many other matters throughout Nature, and seven hundred, and even seven hundred and seventy-seven, human lives have been suggested in some occult and philosophic literature.

Question: How long, on an average, do folk stay in the Spirit World before they reincarnate?

Answer: I have not been able to find any exact information on this subject either. Apparently we are very diverse and vary a great deal in our after-death experiences. In the main, however, there are said to be two chief groups of Egos, if I may call them by that name. One group takes from one thousand to fifteen hundred years between earthly lives, whilst the other takes from five hundred to seven hundred years, and even in those two classifications there are wide variations. If, therefore, you like to take an average of seven hundred years, allowing for the variations, you might not be far wrong.

Of course, this questioner is assuming that Reincarnation is a fact. It does form part of the teachings of Theosophy and knowledge concerning it is based, not upon blind faith, but upon direct occult research carried out, checked and counter-checked by generations of Initiated Seers.

Question: Would you not say that the interval between lives is governed less by the needs of the individual than by the need to keep the world's population constant? It looks as if the Earth's population would be lagging a bit, if there were too many people with fifteen hundred years between their lives!

Answer: I am hardly competent to speak on this matter, which is under the direction of Great Beings concerned with the evolution of the human Race. At present, the Earth's population is increasing regularly by some twenty million people each year, and so I do not think it could be said to be lagging in any way.

With regard to the time period between human lives, this is probably governed by some major law, some great rhythm of Nature to which the evolutionary needs of each individual are adapted. As I stated previously, there are said to be two main groups of Egos or Spiritual Souls of men, one of which takes some fifteen hundred years between lives and the other from five to seven or eight hundred years, wide variation occurring within both groups. Other factors affect these periods. When certain cycles converge, as at present, to make a series of crises on Earth, with all their magnificent opportunities for quickened evolutionary progress, I have heard it taught that as many people as possible are brought into incarnation so that they may benefit from the critical conditions and have a chance of making unusually rapid progress.

Another modification of the period between lives occurs when a certain stage or phase of evolution has been entered, at which the Inner Self is sufficiently strong and developed to be able to take its evolution into its own hands. It can then cause its personality to live so intensely, so vividly and so actively as to make unusually rapid progress in a single life. This entry upon the Path, as it is called, could shorten the number of lives necessary to reach Adeptship. We cannot say with certainty, therefore, how many lives would be needed to achieve this, because the number is subject to modification according to planetary and racial circumstances, and also to alteration by the individual. The number of seven hundred and seventy seven has been hinted at, but this number can presumably be either increased or reduced according to the way the individual lives. Eventually the state of Adeptship is closely approached, and then the necessity for further lives is outgrown.

Question: Examples are given of children and people who remember their past lives, and in our [1] library there are books stated to be the past lives of known people, notably Mr. J. Krishnamurti, and yet you say these are not his [2] past lives. Please explain further.

Answer: The apparent contradiction is largely a matter of words, I think. It is part of the greater problem of: Who is the Self? What am I? Who am

[1] H. P. B. Lodge, Auckland, New Zealand.

[2] By "his" is here meant the named, mortal personality.

I? Are we the familiar, personal identity, with its name, which had a beginning, is growing up—and in some cases old—and which we know very well must have an end, or are we something else? Are we that which is using the body, that mind or thinker who is employing the brain, that something which definitely is not the bodily self but of which, in our higher moments, we become aware? Are we that in us which is time-free and sometimes seems to be all-knowing, from which on occasions there descends a kind of fiery power and knowledge which can make the named person immortal? Theosophy says it is that inner individuality of power and wisdom and fire, the immortal genius within, which is the true Self, and that it is this Inner Self—not the outer man—which reincarnates.

With regard to the book to which the questioner draws attention, the author does not call it *The Lives of Krishnamurti.* He gives the Ego a star name, *Alcyone.* So the book is not a record of the past lives of the Indian philosopher and teacher known to his fellows as Jiddu Krishnamurti, but of the former lives of the fragment of the Divine Self of the Universe of which Jiddu Krishnamurti is a modern manifestation. Actually, each one of us has an Egoic name in addition to this physical name by which we are known down here. This spiritual name is probably a wonderfully beautiful chord, every note of which is expressive of an inherent power and a developed attribute and faculty, a chord or name which is growing fuller and richer as life follows life. It is this, the Inner Ruler Immortal with its spiritual name, which reincarnates.

If I may carry the subject of the Self a little further, from one point of view it is true to say that there is no entirely separate, self-existing, integral Self in man. In each man, as in all that lives, there exists the divine element which is called in *Sanskrit* the *Ātman*, and the *Ātman* of man and the *Ātman* of the universe as a whole are one *Ātman*. Full realisation of this truth is regarded as the highest possible illumination. The Indian *Yogi*, at the culmination of his meditation, proclaims: " The *Ātman* and the *Paramātman* (the Self beyond) are one ", and becomes absorbed, lost in contemplation and experience of that supreme truth.

Question: Do Nations reincarnate, and if so could you please give an illustration?

Answer: Yes, I have heard it said that they do and that some members of that splendid Nation, the Hebrew peoples, tend to keep on reincarnating in their own Race which they come to love so very much.

There is also a kind of occult tradition—and I would stress that none of these ideas are in the least dogmas of the Theosophical Society—that the present French people are in the main reincarnations of the ancient Greeks; also that the Anglo-Saxon Races, in the widest sense of that term, including those in America, are reincarnations of the Roman people. It is possible to trace similarities. For example, the Romans were great colonisers, road-makers, bridge and aquaduct builders. They were also great law-makers, law-givers and lovers of national spectacles. Tens of thousands of people would gather together to see a few perform in the arena. We do the same today in the Anglo-Saxon Nations, though fortunately we do not pit our criminals against each other, against gladiators or against wild beasts. We do gather together, however, in tens of thousands to see two teams of players kicking a ball about! This is more humane and shows that we have progressed, but one can see a similarity between the two peoples in all these things. It seems a feasible idea, then, that the Anglo-Saxons are reincarnations of the ancient Romans. Also, the Prussian Germans are said to be the ancient Carthaginians reborn.

Question: Do you think that Reincarnation and Telepathy have any bearing on the foretelling of the future?

Answer: If you will allow me to say so, I think you are putting three ideas together which are not of the same order, and therefore cannot helpfully be united. The foretelling of the future is less a matter of Telepathy than of a flash of the energy and the consciousness of the Inner Self which temporarily illumines the physical brain.

A simple analogy will help us. A man walking on the ground, perhaps in a hollow, can only see for a limited distance in any direction. His present range of view may be one hundred yards in diameter all around him. Now, a man in an aeroplane three thousand feet or more above the ground could see that walker and the country all round him. The present time of this second person would include both the past and the future of the man below in the hollow. The aeronaut might see thirty miles ahead and thirty miles behind the walker. He would know that if the man goes on walking he will reach a wood, then a bridge, then the main road, then a valley, all of which is in a future that has not yet occurred for the man on the ground. These places are, however, all in the present for the man three thousand feet in the air. So, the Ego may be regarded somewhat as a high flying aeronaut with a far greater range of now-ness and here-ness than the man on the ground. He can see that causes have been set going—such as a certain man walking purposefully in a certain direction—and he will know that in due course resultant effects will follow.

Sometimes a man will receive a flash of this Egoic foreknowledge in his brain, and so know in advance that a particular event will come to pass. This can hardly be referred to as either Reincarnation or Telepathy. Rather is it brain participation in the wider vision of the Inner Self. This pre-knowledge might be telepathically communicated to another person, but Telepathy was hardly its original cause.

2. The Law of Cause and Effect

Question: So many give love and kindness, even self-sacrifice, with no ulterior motive. Why, then, is the return very often one of hatred, especially in the case of relatives?

Answer: If I may say so, I think you ought to say that the *immediate* return can in some cases be hatred. The doctrine of Reincarnation, or successive lives on earth, forms part of the teachings of the Ancient Wisdom and, according to this doctrine, if we cannot find in our present life the causes of our happinesses and our sufferings and pains, then they are to be found in former lives. It is necessary to widen one's outlook and go further back than the present life to discover the initial causes.

Should your relatives dislike, or even hate you, if you look back into your past life relationships with them, when they and you were in other bodies, you will find in your own actions then the sowing of seeds of discord with them, seeds of which the present dislike is a reaping in kind. Admittedly your relatives may be difficult people, but it seems likely that their hatred has an earlier and a deeper origin than your present relationships with them. Then, again, even when performing good deeds and loving actions, wisdom and tact are still necessary. Be careful, therefore, that in putting into practice your ideal of service without reward you are also wise, and above all tactful, in all you try to do for them. Some forms of ministration, even with the best intentions, can become exceedingly irritating!

Question: Does self-inflicted pain fulfil *karma*?

Answer: *Kārmic* effects depend a great deal upon motive. In general I should think the answer would be " No ", but this is a very subtle and difficult question, like many others concerning *karma*. To answer fully, it would be necessary to find out what led up to the state of mind in which a person would inflict pain upon themselves; for a *kārmic* situation cannot ever be completely assessed on one single action alone, because behind every action is a chain of actions and reactions which produced the present individual and their tendencies. So you have to go far back into the past of the person to be able to assess their *kārmic* situation.

I think, however, that one could say that there are three main causes or types of causative action which produce pain. One is cruelty—the infliction of unnecessary pain upon sentient beings. The second is enslavement, including unjust imprisonment. The third is the abuse of one's own body. Ill-treatment and neglect of the body, over-indulgence, as also undue asceticism, the waste of powers, and general misuse of the body and its senses, centres and faculties—these are *kārmic* causes of ill-health and unhappiness.

Self-inflicted pain, then—to answer your question—rather than fulfilling *karma*, as you put it, would be more likely to generate fresh adversity. Do not forget, however, that the opposite is also true. Right care of the body and the intelligent use of its powers generate health and happiness.

Question: Will the environment in this world in the future be suitable for those who reincarnate with much back *karma* to be worked off ?

Answer: I wonder if you mean back *karma* or bad *karma*? All *karma* could be described as back *karma*, since the generating causes must always precede the experience of their effects. If you mean bad *karma*, I know you are referring to restrictive and pain-producing effects of discordant and cruel conduct. A philosopher, however, would not allow us to speak of " bad " *karma*, since all *karma* is educative and corrective, and is therefore beneficial or "good" in its ultimate effect. The answer to your question is, I think, "absolutely suitable". We need have no slightest doubt about this matter. The law is marvellously accurate in its outworking, even down to the smallest possible degree. As Our Lord said: "Judge not, that ye be not judged. For with what judgment ye judge, ye shall be judged; and with what measure ye mete, it shall be measured to you again." (*Matt.* VII: 1, 2). At all times and on all occasions one's environment is completely suitable, as you put it—I would rather say perfectly adapted—to the working out of both national and individual *karma*.

Question: A man, through his selfishness, has brought much suffering to others and he has escaped punishment. Should another give the word which would bring some measure of punishment to him? What of the person so doing?

Answer: That is a question, surely, which only you yourself can answer. Can you be sure, however, that he has escaped punishment? Is it not too soon as yet to say that? Would you not rather say that he *appears* to have escaped punishment up to now? There is an old Portuguese proverb which says: "God permits, but not for ever." Theosophists might say that the law permits, but not for ever. As St. Paul said: "God is not mocked: for whatsoever a man soweth, that shall he also reap." (*Gal.* VI: 7). To that statement by the Apostle the Theosophist might wish respectfully to add, "If not in the same life, then in lives which follow after." Our Lord also stated: "And it is easier for heaven and earth to pass, than one tittle of the law to fail." (*Luke* XVI: 17). Thus, however long delayed, retribution, nemesis, will inevitably overtake the wrongdoer.

Are you to be the agent of retribution? That is your problem. I cannot solve it for you or any other person. I see the difficulty. Sometimes the law does *seem* to fail. The effects do not always appear in the same life in which the causes are generated, but you may be perfectly sure that God is not mocked and that what this man—as all men—sows, that shall he and they also reap. Perhaps, then, you might let the matter rest there, particularly if no continuance or cruelty is involved.

If, however, you press me, I think I would say, "No, do not yourself bring the offender to justice." I think it could be inadvisable. If you have any means of approach to this person, advise, warn, in the wisest, sanest, most tactful and most convincing way possible, and leave the situation there. It is not impossible, remember, that by interference, even with the best motives, you would arouse greater anger and cruelty in the person.

Go to the aid of the victims, for that would be a more constructive and useful line of conduct.

Question: Is there much credit given to the person who endeavours to live a good life wholly with a view to the attainment of everlasting bliss and avoidance of future suffering?

Answer: The way in which this question is phrased, if I might be allowed to say so, is somewhat misleading. The questioner asks, "Is there much credit given to the person. . . .?" There is no giving of credit by anyone to anyone. The concept of a sort of personal Deity Who parcels out favours according to His own idea of things is not, I understand, very acceptable to the mind of the philosopher, who seems to prefer the concept of a strictly impersonal law. God, for the spiritual philosopher, is primarily law, so that it is not a question of credit being meted out or withheld—it is purely a matter of cause and effect. A ball thrown against a wall will bounce back and the distance to which it will bounce, as also the direction and everything else that happens to it—all these things are governed by certain laws of dynamics, which are strictly impersonal. So, also, as far as my understanding of it goes, is *karma* or the law of action and reaction. To follow up the questioner's thought, motive, it is truly said, does play a decisive part so far as effects of actions are concerned. Indeed, motive can be more decisive than the action itself.

Let us take, for example, the case of Jack the Ripper, a criminal who many years ago went about certain districts in London at night attacking lonely wayfarers. With his knife he ripped open the abdomens of a great number of people in a whole series of murders. Now, a surgeon performs that very action continually for most of his life, but how different the motive! The surgeon seeks to heal and to help and it is that inner motive which is decisive in determining the *kārmic* effect.

As to the process of doing good wholly with a view to personal spiritual reward, that selfish motive would reduce the beneficent effects of the good life and the good deeds. By example and precept Our Lord Christ called upon us to display the uttermost unselfishness, serving always without thought of reward. According to His teaching, if a person seeks to borrow something give him twice what he asks; if he asks you to walk a mile with him, go two; if he wants your coat give him your cloak also and selflessly, as a ministration of love. In this statement of the ideal, unselfishness is carried much further. Not only is there to be no motive of gain, but more than that; for generous self-giving, even if it involves personal loss, is inculcated.

So, also, counselled the Lord Buddha. He taught that the first step towards Buddhahood consisted of the birth within the mind of the thought of attaining enlightenment for the sake of others. Until that thought dawned in the mind, He stated, the possibility of reaching Nirvana did not actively exist, though ever inherent within the Monad, the Divine Spark, the Dweller in the Innermost. All through both Buddhism and Hinduism one finds the teaching that one should never seek Nirvana—eternal blessedness—for personal benefit; for that very motive would bar the way to conscious absorption in the Spiritual Soul of the Universe, the highest state of spiritual bliss in absolute immortality. Thus it would seem that the motive for action which brings the greatest credit, as you put it (I would rather say the most beneficent, long-term effects), is that of spontaneously doing good for good's sake, for love's sake, and without thought of return.

3. The Karma of Nations

Question: Can you explain the hundreds of years of misery which India has suffered?

Answer: In the light of *karma* it must be neither illogical nor unjust. Even if you visited India and learned to love, respect and reverence that great Motherland and the spirit of her people, nevertheless if you studied her history and watched the current conduct of her life, you would find that which is discordant. The same is, of course, also true of all peoples, but in India you would find a large percentage of illiterates, past and present inflictions of cruelty, and animal sacrifices in some forms of temple worship. These practices, continuing century after century can reasonably be seen, I think, as some of the contributory causes of India's sufferings under the law of cause and effect.

Remember, also, that India is a Nation which long ago entered upon the declining arc of her national existence; for here the law of cycles operates. All Nations have their inception or beginning, followed generally by a pioneering phase, in its turn followed by the establishment of culture, education, the sciences and the arts and an ordered form of government. Whilst still on the upward arc, greater heights—especially in religion and the arts—are reached, as also in the general beauty of national life and national living. Eventually the peak is attained in the establishment of the finest type of government and the highest form of religion of which the Nation is capable. This may be sustained for many centuries, or even millennia, but under the cyclic law a decline inevitably sets in.

This decline is also contributed to by the departure of those advanced Egos who have raised up the Nation, for they must go to other lands to build up great Nations there. Less highly evolved Egos then come in, to benefit by sharing in a high civilisation which they could not have produced for themselves. They cannot, however, maintain that level, and deterioration begins. They in their turn are followed by still less evolved Souls, who are aided by what still remains of high culture. Inevitably the decline continues, so that at last the cycle of descent is complete, sometimes resulting in the disappearance of the Nation, its people and its culture. India does not seem to have reached the end of her national greatness, however, as have ancient Egypt, Persia, Assyria, Chaldea, Greece and Rome. Far from it; for it would seem that India has now entered upon a new cycle of national existence, a new round of her spiral ascent to greatness. Indeed an Indian statesman, as reported in the New Zealand Press in January, 1952, stated that India could in ten years abolish most of her miseries. Should she succeed, with her wealth of spirituality, philosophy, culture and her Scriptures she could make a priceless contribution to the progress of humanity.

4. Predestination and Free Will

Question: What becomes of *karma* if the Masters direct individuals or Nations?

Answer: The Masters inspire rather than direct. They are not rulers of fate in the sense of being almighty. They shed a spiritualising influence abroad and They direct only in the sense of offering inspiration. Even as in the Biblical story the rich young ruler was left free, so are all Nations and all men. (*Matt.* XIX: 16-23). Furthermore, the Masters cannot violate *kārmic* law. Even the Lord "could there do no mighty work . . . because of their unbelief." (*Mark* VI: 5, 6). If, then, Nations are helped by the Masters of the Wisdom, it is because their *karma* permits it. Profound and complex issues are, however, involved in the operation of *kārmic* law. The receipt of proffered help, as also the capacity to respond, are two of them, but I cannot on this occasion go more fully into those aspects of the subject.

Question: Can a Third World War be prevented by the Lord of the World?

Answer: It is not for me to say what so mighty a Being as the Supreme Ruler of Evolution upon this globe, Earth's Spiritual King, can or cannot do. I assume the answer would be, "Yes, most certainly." It is not a question, however, of what He *can* do, but of the wisest course to follow and of the working out of the law of cause and effect. These are amongst the decisive factors. Even in intervention in the affairs of the world They, the Mighty Ones, cannot on behalf of others contravene the operation of the inviolable law of cause and effect. If a Third World War be within the *karma* of humanity, though every effort be made, it cannot by phenomenal means and force, as far as I understand it, be stayed.

The great movement to produce a United Nations of the World is surely inspired by the Elder Brethren of Humanity—that is one of Their ways of trying to prevent a Third World War. They inspire humanity to recognise Brotherhood and to unite for world peace. They flood the World-Mind with a vision of light and life and beauty and unity. By such means, rather than by some occult phenomenon, the Lord of the World and His Hierarchy of Adepts seek to save us from ourselves and, it would appear, despite ourselves.

As far as man is concerned, this ministration by the Elder Brethren of Humanity thus takes many forms. Mankind is helped in every department of life—individual, national and international. Man's deepest and most sacred aspirations are inspired and fostered by Them. The flash of inspiration which comes to the great scientist after years of patient experimenting, revealing to him the theory or the law he tried to find out; the illumination and experience of a great truth coming to the philosopher in the silence of his contemplation;

the vision of beauty seen by the artist and embodied in his work; the purity of the saint and the power of the magician or priest, as also the fiery enthusiasm of the reformer—all these receive stimulus and inspiration from appropriate Adept Officials.

Superhuman Beings also influence world affairs in general by: a ceaseless intellectual pressure towards idealism; the direct projection of seed-thoughts, principles, ideas; perpetually shedding intellectual light, product of Their own illumination, into the thought world; strengthening, even stiffening, the morale of every good man and woman, and especially idealists and leaders of beneficent national and world Movements; direct intervention whenever the evolutionary movement and the well-being of Nations and individuals render it desirable and possible; taking and training Disciples into Initiates, and Initiates into Adepts; founding such Movements as the Theosophical Society, designed to shed the light of knowledge into the mind of man.

The Fraternity is relatively small in number. Each Initiate and Adept is as a catalytic agent on the planes of pure will, wisdom, intuition and intellect. Moreover, when an Adept arises from the ranks of the Initiates of this planet, human evolution is quickened, the whole of humanity being then lifted nearer to its goal. Indeed, the whole of manifested Life in the four kingdoms of Nature receives an evolutionary quickening.

The innumerable individual Adept activities designed to these ends differ according to the necessities of the times, the special tasks entrusted to the Elder Brothers of the Race, and the Office held in the Hierarchy of Initiates and Adepts.

Question: Why should the slothful individual make a special effort when the final goal is *determined* ?

Answer: For the sake of others. They *need* not make a special effort. All men are free to delay, leave unaffected or hasten the speed of their evolutionary progress. Every step forward that a single individual takes, however, makes the way a little easier for all who follow, makes smoother their path, brings light to the minds of the rest of mankind. That is the motive, that is the purpose of treading the Path, as it is called. Our Lord expressed the inspiration which carries every aspirant through Gethsemane and Golgotha to the triumphant Ascension in His words: "And I, if I be lifted up from the earth, will draw all men unto me." (*John* XII: 32).

The questioner speaks of the slothful individual hurrying or hastening on the way. Such people are not likely to do so, because they are not yet fully awakened to the existence of the Way, otherwise they would not be slothful. They are not yet conscious of the pressure of the Life-Force within them, otherwise there would be no sloth. When once that realisation comes, when once that mysterious, inner change occurs which sets the Soul on fire for evermore, then—and this, perhaps, is the *real* answer to your question—they seek and tread the Path *because they cannot help themselves.* They are impelled from within to the highest they know. As the mountaineer aspires to the summit and the explorer to the Pole, so, in the words of an Eastern Scripture, for the spiritually awakened " there is no other Path at all to go." (*Kathopanishad*).

Author's Note: Since, owing to the need for brevity, the above answer deals rather incompletely with the complex problem of predestination and free will, I here add some further personal views.

The subject of predestination and free will has deeply occupied the minds of scholars and students. Part of the theosophical contribution to the solution of the apparent paradox would seem to be that there are at least two universal forces at work upon man under which he is virtually powerless. One of these is evolutionary pressure at all levels of his existence from within outwards such as that, for example, which, physically applied, produces an oak from an acorn. The other force perpetually resolves into harmony all discordant conditions, continually corrects imbalance.

The principle of unfoldment under the irresistible pressure of a propellant energy operates from within the innermost essence of the universe and the spiritual seeds or germs (Monads) of all beings. The process of the maintenance of harmony is ceaselessly active throughout the universe and all it contains. This harmonisation operates upon man as a sequence of cause and effect, under which discordances created by his selfish and cruel actions, for example, are forcibly resolved and harmony is restored.

These two powers—unfoldment from less to more and re-harmonisation—operate irresistibly upon man, as upon all else that exists. Man can delay or hasten, but he cannot ultimately frustrate these two functions of the Cosmic Will. The operation of the universal law of cyclic expansion and evolution is irresistible. In these two natural processes man is helpless, in them predestined. In due course man as Monad must reach the stature of perfected and harmonised manhood. Similarly every human action, modified by subsequent actions, will inevitably bring about an exactly appropriate reaction upon the actor. In this man is indeed powerless, and so predestined.

This predestination need not in the least disturb the minds of those who become aware of it, for the simple reason that the two inner impulses—to expand and to harmonise—arise from within the Spirit-Self of man, which is identical with the Spirit-Self of the universe. Once the concept is removed of an external, controlling Deity separate from man, the sense of compulsion then vanishes; for if man is predestined, then he is self-predestined, which removes all stigma from the fact. If man's future is predetermined, then he himself is the only predeterminator and, moreover, is predestined by the action of his own free will.

Perfect happiness is utterly certain for him if he voluntarily collaborates with these two Cosmic procedures—perpetual unfoldment and the maintenance of harmony. The man who orders his life to the end of the most harmonious and speedy evolutionary progress at all levels will generate no friction, and so find peace. The man who always acts harmoniously, never unnecessarily injuring any other being, and who within himself is ever harmonious and a harmoniser—he is assured of freedom from the painful re-attuning process. He does not provoke the retaliation of the law. Ever deepening harmony and happiness will be his. A Greek proverb says: "He who is obedient to the law the Gods lead gently by the hand. Those who resist, They drive mercilessly."

Thus, though fundamentally self-predestined, restriction and suffering are by no means inevitably pre-ordained for man. He creates them for himself and he can, therefore, do away with them for himself. In these ways man can be free and the Great Teachers who have visited mankind have, by both example and precept, shown him the way of freedom.

The problem of predestination and free will may perhaps thus be regarded, and the apparent paradox which they seem to present be partially resolved.

PART THREE

SUPERPHYSICAL BEINGS AND STATES OF CONSCIOUSNESS

1. THE LIFE AFTER DEATH

Question: We know the Life-Force is indestructible, but surely you must admit that, beyond the scientific fact that the material body decays after death, man has not the knowledge of any other phenomenon and therefore *his* idea of the life after death can only be surmise and is not based on *scientific* truth?

Answer: I do not know whether that attitude, which is a natural one to adopt, is really tenable today. So much progress has been made in the study of the supernormal powers and faculties of man, so much has been demonstrated concerning their existence, that it would be a brave person nowadays who would put a limit to the possible range of human awareness and powers of research. Certainly I would not do so myself.

I feel positive—nay, I know—that there are those who possess extra-sensory powers and who are able to enter and to investigate the world of the life after death, for example. They are then able to check and counter-check their findings with those of other investigators, and thus to provide themselves with exact knowledge of after-death conditions. I would suggest to the questioner, therefore, that he read and make a general study of the subject of Para-psychology. There is a monthly *Journal of Para-psychology* issued by the Duke University, also one by the London University, I think, dealing with supernormal vision and the fruits of its exercise. *New Frontiers of the Mind*, by Dr. J. B. Rhine (Penguin Series), is an exposition of extra-sensory perception or ESP. Theosophical literature on this subject, much of which is based upon occult research, is replete with information upon these matters. Whilst *post-mortem* existence can hardly be demonstrated, it can be proven for himself by an occult investigator.

Question: Would you say with confidence that those who have entered into the new world (of the life after death) can see us from there as we are in this life?

Answer: Not entirely, I understand. In the first awakening from the unconsciousness which follows death and the review (of the life just closed, which occurs at death), and also in some cases of sudden death, yes, the deceased seem still to have the faculty of seeing physical objects and human physical bodies, or what we wrongly call "ourselves". They can also see the inner man, as well as the Soul of things, and so they see our hearts and minds as objective phenomena. They can tell what we are thinking, striving for, going through. They can share our interests and joys, and far more intimately than was possible down here, save in rare circumstances. Yes, I am confident that they do know and see us, especially immediately after death, though perhaps not as we are now seeing each other physically, but far more truly as we *really* are.

Question: What is the effect in the next world of evil living while on Earth?

Answer: Let me take one case as an example. Let us consider what happens to those who pass away in the grip of some unconquered vice—alcoholism, for instance. After death, when external awareness returns such people are just as they were before, except that the physical body has gone. They are functioning in what is called the emotional body—the body in which the emotions arise and are objectively visible in colour. In that body of desire their natural and acquired feelings are very apparent to them. If, then, there is a craving for some material, sensual pleasure the deceased are in a parlous state, for the craving is now experienced with an added intensity but with no possibility of its gratification.

Desire and sensual cravings are not limited to the physical cells, as is generally supposed. They arise and are first experienced in the desire body, the so-called astral body, which is the vehicle of emotion and without which no physical sensation would be possible. After death, human consciousness is at first largely limited to the astral plane and the astral body, in which the *kāmic* (*Sk.*), or desire principle, inheres. In consequence, there can be very considerable suffering after death. People do die under these conditions, and if there be a Hell at all, then it is this—the condition of the individual who is a prey to passions and has lost all power to gratify them.

Such a Hell, if I may use the term, differs from the orthodox Christian theological conception of Hell—though not that common to Hinduism and Buddhism—in several ways. First of all it is not a place, a location, but a state of consciousness, as also is Heaven, and in this sense one can be in either Heaven or Hell wherever one is. Furthermore, *post-mortem* suffering is not the result of a judgment from outside or above. It is not a penal award. It is self-created, as is all suffering and all happiness under the impersonal law of cause and effect.

The experience is neither valueless nor wasted; for the intensity of the suffering is so great that it burns itself into the Soul, the Inner Ego, and registers itself indelibly within the consciousness. When such a person is reborn they will feel an instinctual repugnance to certain kinds of indulgence. So there *is* suffering, but progress, development and expansion are achieved as a result of these and other experiences in the life after death.

Lastly, this kind of suffering is never eternal. Occult investigation does not support the illogical idea that eternal damnation could be the consequence of sins committed *in time*. There are no finally lost Spiritual Souls, whatever may happen to the *psyche* or mento-emotional nature of man. By its very nature the Soul, meaning the Inner, Spiritual Triad, is eternal, immortal, indestructible. In addition, there is no place in the Cosmos in which a Soul could be utterly and eternally lost, isolated for evermore. There is no region where the Divine Life is not present, no place where the Divine Love does not enfold all beings, no condition in which the Everlasting Arms are not always underneath. Every life is a guarded and guided life and every one of us, no matter how low we may seem to fall, is still dear to the Heart of Being. Perhaps in our weaknesses and our falls we are even nearer and dearer to God's love than before. Be that as it may, we are all helped continually, both from without and within, to rise from our weaknesses, to learn the lessons which they teach. All our sufferings, including those after death, only last as long as the energy lasts which we have put into the causative errors and indulgences. Even a human father would not be so cruel and illogical as to condemn a son to eternal punishment for a sin committed in time. The pain passes, the enflamed astral condition cools down, the vice is conquered, and the Soul at last wins free. A great lesson has been learnt and much progress made towards the fulfilment of the goal of human existence, which is evolution to the stature of perfected manhood.

Question: What of those who have lived evil, cruel lives? Have they nothing to fear after death?

Answer: They have much to fear in both the life after death and the physical lives which will follow. If they have not lived cruel lives, they need fear neither death nor what follows after. Death is a perfectly natural procedure and need not be anticipated with the slightest apprehension. The passage through the gateway of Death is nearly always made unconsciously.

Question: What happens after death to those who commit suicide?

Answer: There are three main types of suicide, each with its own characteristic *post-mortem* experiences. There are those who take their lives to help or to honour others. Such people pass through the same experiences as they would have done if they had died from sudden death. They are instantly awake and, apart from the shock, continue under the conditions which I have just described in my lecture. (*Vide Through the Gateway of Death*, Geoffrey Hodson).

Others who commit suicide take their lives in order to escape from unbearable experiences. When these die, they pass into blank unconsciousness in the inner worlds and remain there in a mento-astral coma of darkness, as it were, losing evolutionary time so far as the personal nature is concerned. Eventually a rather strange thing happens. When the time of natural death comes round, by some law of rhythm those who commit this type of suicide awaken from slumber and resume, or take up, the *post-mortem* life under the laws and conditions to which I have referred.

A third type consists of those who take their lives in a fit of passion. They have a very unenviable time. They cannot enter into the higher worlds. They cannot get away from the physical world, but can still see it. They are in a half world, as it were, driven by their own passions from which they try to escape, but cannot. They are earth-bound, and in some cases seek vicarious gratifications of their desires by obsessing physical persons who are indulging in some form of excessive sensuality. Their condition is tragic. Help is available to all—under an organised system of ministration everyone is assisted—but to commit suicide is always a mistake, whatever the motive. It is far better to live the trouble through. Then the debt is paid instead of being carried on to a future life, when it will have been complicated by the preceding act of self-murder. Occult investigation shows, as I have said, that suicide is always a mistake.

2. Dreams

Question: What causes dreams, sometimes horrible and sometimes of events which are impossible in physical life?

Answer: There are many different kinds of dreams, some of which have purely physical causes. These may be of two types, those due to external causes and those due to interior, bodily changes. A noise in the room, a draught of wind, rain, movement in the house—these, for example, can start a dream process. Also, changes in the temperature of the body, chemical action, blood pressure, digestive processes and so on, cause certain kinds of dreams.

Another type consists of dreams which are symbolical and expressive of conditions in the *psyche* or Soul. Such dreams are often very illuminating and helpful to diagnosis inphysical, mental or emotional troubles, or all three. These may reach waking consciousness as fearful and, as the questioner says, horrible dreams. Psychological well-being and harmony may be presented to the brain-mind in the form of pleasant, happy dreams. Sometimes physical conditions, experiences and needs reach us on waking as dramatic symbols which have their own meaning, or as shapes, colours, odours or members of the sub-human kingdoms of Nature, all of which are symbolical and have meanings personal to the dreamer.

Then there is a further class of dream which is a memory, sometimes confused and at other times clear, of actual experiences of the Inner Self during the body's unconsciousness in sleep; for when we are free of the physical body whilst it sleeps we travel about in a subtler vehicle, and with varying degrees of awareness, in the inner, superphysical worlds.

We do not normally remember these activities, but we do pass through them. On waking, they sometimes reach the brain, less as dreams than as memories of events that have actually occurred. We may also bring through premonitions of future events which are later recorded in the Press, and then we know them as having been real, superphysical experiences.

The questioner's horrible dreams, therefore, may be expressive of psychological maladjustment, of disequilibrium, of some adverse influence in home or surroundings, or of some occult experiences passed through during the hours of the night. By examining them, or having them examined by a skilled interpreter, one may find out their meaning and derive considerable benefit from the knowledge.

3. Guardian Angels

Question: What is a Guardian Angel? Is there an esoteric significance to this phrase?

Answer: A Guardian Angel is a member of the Angelic Hosts—but is not necessarily permanently attached to one person. There is in operation a principle of guardianship which is a universal expression of a conserving principle in Nature which might be termed the Love of God. That principle finds its manifestation both in human beings who become protectors of those in need, and in members of the Angelic Hosts who do the same. The Angels are the incarnation of impersonality. When an occasion arises for guardianship, some member of the Angelic Hosts observes it and, within the limits of the law, guards and protects that particular person. On another occasion it could be a different member of the Angelic Hosts who similarly assisted.

There is one exception to that rule, however, and this information is offered not the least dogmatically, but as the shared fruits of research, as something worth thinking over. Special links are made with Orders of Angels, and even with individual members of those Orders, by men and women who have been admitted, either in former incarnations or in the present life, to certain "valid" Ceremonial Orders such as Freemasonry and the Lesser and Greater Mysteries. When, for example, the Rite or Sacrament of Baptism is performed within Denominations of the Christian Church which are in the Apostolic Succession, one of the effects is to associate for the rest of that life a member of the Angelic Hosts—not a deceased human being, by the way—with the person who is baptized. This being is said not to be a highly evolved Angel, but a sylph which has some affinity with the Soul and nature of the person baptized. These two are brought together by the Rite of Baptism, and in that case there is some form of guardianship and helpfulness by one particular Angel for one particular person.

Knowledge of the principle of guardianship can be used most effectively. Human thought is very powerful and can be either hurtful or helpful, danger-producing or protective. If, for instance, we have a friend or loved one in conditions of danger, perhaps a soldier in battle, our daily thoughts of him as being safe are as prayers to the Higher Powers that he may be protected. These thoughts assume radiant forms, concentrations of thought-force, perhaps like winged spheres—rosy wings and golden balls of light—and they flash off to where the person is, hover in the neighbourhood nearby and gradually discharge some of their force into the aura of that person, steadying them, making them more cautious, and establishing a better relationship between Ego and brain. Then, should there be a moment when to step in one direction would mean death, and in another direction life, this thought-force would helpfully influence such a person.

In addition to this, we can also invoke the aid of the Angelic Hosts by such an invocation as: "May the power and the love of God bless and protect—mentioning Christian and surname—and may the Guardian Angels encompass them." Make a clear mental image of God's enveloping Love and of encompassing Angel Presences. Do this regularly each day, always with a surrender to the Divine Will and Law, then you can really protect those in possible danger both by your thought-forces and by the invocation of Guardian Angels. My books, *The Brotherhood of Angels and of Men* and *The Kingdom of the Gods*, deal with this subject.

PART FOUR

ADEPTSHIP AND THE ADEPTS

1. The Adept Brotherhood and World Affairs

Question: Who were some of the wise Teachers to whom you referred in your lecture?

Answer: They were and are Members of the great Company of the Adept Sages whose names are to be found in history. The greatest of Them, of course, are the Founders of the World Faiths, beginning in our historical epoch and just before it with Hermes in Egypt, Zoroaster in Persia and Orpheus in Greece. In India the succession was continued by the appearance of the great Lord Vyasa, Shri Krishna, Shri Shankaracharya and Lord Buddha. Then, amongst the very greatest, and thought by some to be the Teacher of Teachers, was the Lord Christ who appeared in Palestine 2,000 years ago. Only less great are the philosophers and sages, particularly those of the period from 600 B.C. to 400 A.D.—a wonderful epoch in world history.

Amongst these in the East were Confucius and Lao Tzu, and in the West Plato, Pythagoras, Aristotle, Socrates, Porphyry, Plotinus, the Alexandrian philosophers and the Gnostic Fathers, all of whom have shed upon the world the light of the Ancient Wisdom and age by age, with one voice, have revealed its truths. Today, also, there are great philosophers and teachers in the world, although the present, perhaps, is rather an age of mental, intellectual, inventive, mechanical and scientific developments than of spiritual and philosophic revelation. Nevertheless, great minds still shed their light upon the world, although that light may only be fully appreciated by later generations of men.

Although it was not a part of the answer to the foregoing question, I include the following Hymn[1] expressive of the concept of a universal Wisdom Religion brought to the world by Adept Teachers, of which each World Faith is a partial expression:

> Gather us in, Thou Love that fillest all,
> Gather our rival faiths within Thy fold;
> Rend each man's temple's veil, and bid it fall,
> That we may know that Thou hast been of old.

[1] Rev. G. Matheson, 1842-1906. No. 295, *The St. Albans Hymnal*, The Liberal Catholic Church. Tune, Consolation or St. Agnus (Langrin).

Gather us in; we worship only Thee;
In varied names we stretch a common hand,
In diverse forms a common soul we see;
In many ships we seek one spirit-land.

Thine is the mystic life great India craves,
Thine is the Parsi's purifying beam,
Thine is the Buddhist's rest from tossing waves,
Thine is the empire of vast China's dream.

Thine is the Roman's strength without his pride,
Thine is the Greek's glad world without its slaves,
Thine is Judea's law, with love beside,
Truth that enlightens, charity that saves.

Each sees one colour of Thy rainbow light,
Each looks upon one tint and calls it heaven;
Thou art the fullness of our partial sight;
We are not perfect till we find the seven.

Some seek a Father in the heavens above;
Some ask a human image to adore;
Some crave a spirit vast as life and love;
Within Thy mansions we have all and more.

O glorious Triune God, embracing all,
By many Paths do men approach Thy Throne;
All Paths are Thine; Thou hearest every call;
Each earnest seeker has Thee for his own.

Question: Could you please describe to us the physical appearance of the Adepts?

Answer: There are descriptions in our theosophical literature by those rare and highly privileged people who are said actually to have seen Members of the Adept Fraternity. One such book I would recommend to you is *The Masters and the Path* by

C. W. Leadbeater, who is regarded by some as one of the greatest seers and occultists of this century. The questioner may there read the author's descriptions of certain Masters of the Wisdom.

I can only briefly, and with humility and reverence, repeat part of what he says. The Adepts are nearly all of Them taller than normal human stature, which gives Them grace, and even majesty. Their faces are said to be unusually handsome, the brow lofty, broad and noble, the eyes large and lit with an inner fire and divine power, yet at times full of humour and glowing with friendliness, kindness and compassion. They are said to have conquered death and to be able to maintain Their physical bodies in youthful maturity for a longer period than is normal for mankind. They live in retreat in different parts of the world, in certain cases in the fastnesses of mountain chains. Some, it is said, live in the remote country of Tibet in or near the Altai Himalaya, some on the slopes of the Himalayas, some in the mountains of Southern India, some in Lebanon and others in the Valley of the Nile and elsewhere. For the most part They remain hidden from a humanity which, in ignorance, might interfere with Their beneficent activities.

Great, glorious and loving Elder Brothers are They, not further away because They are so great and so far beyond mankind, but nearer because of Their attainment. One of the ways in which They minister is that They never leave unanswered a prayer for wisdom in order to be more helpful to others. No Soul ever sends out a genuine, ardent cry for light, wisdom, understanding, knowledge—especially if the motive is to serve—without that cry being heard and answered. This answering of the call of human hearts for light is one of Their many ministrations to mankind. If the seeker responds, they will later be led to the wisdom and to the knowledge which they need. If they persevere, they may be drawn into the very presence of the particular Teacher or Master who is awaiting each and every one of us. Thereafter they may, if they wish, enter the Path of Discipleship—an inestimable privilege.

Question: Those Superhuman People who came here—are They still here? Still active? Did They come in Spirit only, or in physical space ships? From what planet did They come? Or what star?

Answer: Thank you for a series of interesting questions. To all of them Theosophy offers fairly clear-cut answers, not dogmatically in any way, but only as food for thought.

Are They still here, these Seniors of this present world humanity? Some of Them have remained. At least four of the great Adepts stayed and some of the human beings who accompanied Them. When the Earth humanity began to produce its own Initiates and Adepts, as it did in the Fourth Root Race, the work performed by the august Visitors was handed over to Them. Some of those Beings from another planet then gradually withdrew, possibly to undertake similar work on other planets. So we learn that from that first group of Adepts who came here from Venus over six million years ago, there has gradually developed the present Occult Hierarchy of Adepts and Initiates who constitute the Inner or Spiritual Government of the World.

So far as Their physical bodies are concerned, as I have just said the Adepts of our Earth live in retreat, either in the fastnesses of mountain chains or with Their residences protected from a humanity which, through lack of understanding, might render more difficult Their ministrations to mankind. Their consciousness is completely free of Their physical bodies, which They can leave and re-enter at will. It does not matter, therefore, where the body is, for the Adept who uses it can be aware, active and, if desirable, physically visible at any place on the planet as becomes necessary for the fulfilment of His task.

Did They come to the Earth from Their home, the planet Venus, in Spirit only or in physical space ships, you ask. They are said to have come in Their superphysical bodies, and the greatest of Them then formed perfect physical bodies by Their power of will and thought, whilst others took incarnation amongst Earth's humanity of that time, which greatly helped the evolution of the Race. I am aware that this must sound strange to those for whom it is new, but please remember that theosophical teaching is only offered to us for our consideration, as food for thought.

The very highest of the Venusian Adepts who were able to create bodies by the action of Their will and Their thought, by *yoga* in fact, are in consequence sometimes referred to in occult books, notably *The Secret Doctrine* by H. P. Blavatsky, as "The Sons of Will and Yoga". These bodies never change, are not subject to birth and death, always retaining their original youthful appearance. Such hidden powers of the mind, and the capacity of the mind to influence physical matter, are now being investigated. Some scientists are examining extra-sensory perception—chiefly telepathy, clairvoyance and clairaudience—whilst others are studying what is called telekinesis, or the power of the mind to influence physical matter. One of the tests which has given evidence of the existence of this power in man concerned the capacity to influence the fall of dice by concentrated thought.

A power can and will be developed by later Races which will enable man to move and shape matter by the action of his thought alone. Even today some people can make suspended needles swing by the power of their thought, and there is mention of such powers in the great Scriptures of the world. Elisha, for example, made an axe-head float. Christ walked on the water and stilled a storm by the sheer power of His conjoined will and thought and voice. Thus, it is not altogether incredible that the extremely highly evolved Beings of whom we have been thinking could materialise bodies by the power of Will-Thought, or *kriyāshakti*, as it is called in *Sanskrit* by Hindu occultists.

In reply to your other question—"From what planet did They come?"—the answer is that They came, as I have been saying, from the planet Venus, whose Planetary Scheme is almost one and a half Chains in advance of the one to which we belong, namely the Earth Planetary Scheme. The average humanity of Venus must therefore be presumed to be at least at the level of our Initiates, and the more advanced at the level of Earth's Adepts. To those who wish to study this subject in detail, I would recommend the books, *Man: Whence; How and Whither* by Dr. Besant and C. W. Leadbeater, and *The Solar System* by A. E. Powell. There you will find much information about evolution on other planets, the arrival on Earth many ages ago of the Lords of the Flame from Venus, and the different Races of men on this our Globe.

When considering racial evolution upon Earth it should be remembered that the same spiritual individuals, the same human Egos, incarnate in successive Races. The Atlanteans, Egyptians and other ancient peoples were none other than ourselves in our former lives. Similarly, the Sixth sub-Race of our Aryan, or Fifth Root Race, and the Sixth and Seventh Root Races, will only be new reincarnations of the same family of Egos, ourselves, for whom this Earth has been appointed as the evolutionary field.

Question: Could you give us any known instances of direct Adept intervention in national and international affairs within the last few hundred years?

Answer: Yes, I will give you one or two. But remember that this is only a proffered theosophical idea, not a dogma affirmed from our platform. There are not any such in our Society.

What was one of the great keys to our victory in the last War? What preserved the life lines between Britain, India and Egypt? What was so valuable that the enemy made every effort to capture or destroy it and we made every effort to preserve it, and against increasing difficulties? It was the Island of Malta, one of the most important Islands in the world from a strategic point of view.

Look into the history of Malta. There the Knights of Malta, or the Knights of the Order of St. John of Jerusalem, established their Order and beautiful Temple. You will find presiding over them at a certain critical time in world history a being called Ferdinand von Hompesch, who is traditionally identified with one of the Adepts. He, with the appearance of cowardice, surrendered Malta without a fight to the French, and when Napoleon was defeated Malta came into the hands of the British, and it has remained in their hands ever since. There is an occult tradition that the change was engineered by the Great Brotherhood.

Then there was that strange being who presented himself at the time when the U.S.A. was forming its Constitution and designing its flag. A book entitled *Our Flag* by R. A. Campbell, describes the people present at these two activities which brought the Union into existence. This person was called the Professor. Nobody seems to have known his name. He is described as of a commanding presence, dignified, courteous and gracious, so much so that all present, including Franklin, Lynch, Harrison and General Washington, paid him immediate deference. He was the guest of a lady of Boston, at whose home they gathered to design the flag and the Constitution and to determine whether they would break free, which he, with a flow of oratory, adjured them to do. This they did.

Such attempts by Adepts and Their agents to influence world events do not always succeed. The Comte de St. Germain tried to stop the French Revolution and failed. He was called the "Mysterious Wonder Man of Europe", endowed with the most remarkable powers, the friend of Kings and Queens, welcomed at the Courts of Europe. He pleaded with Marie Antoinette and King Louis XVI (1764-93) to accede to the demands of the people and to save a national volcanic eruption—for royalty and aristocracy were sitting on the volcano of the bitterness of a repressed people. They declined, and the volcano erupted in the form of the French Revolution.

That is an interesting case of apparent Adept failure. They may not force mankind; They may only inspire and advise. If you will look into history you will find many cases of such intervention. I commend to you a book entitled *The Comte de St. Germain* by Isabel Cooper Oakley—a thrilling book containing references from the archives of the Courts of Europe and giving glimpses of the strange powers of these, the Supermen of our Earth.

Question: Would Adepts (or near-Adepts) have the powers to trace, for instance, missing persons, and if so why do They not offer Their services in so practical a way in order to alleviate in some measure the sufferings of humanity?

Answer: Which is better—to save from suffering in a single case or to teach a principle and a truth which, if accepted, would save from sorrow all mankind? That is the problem; for, great though the work and the powers of the Adepts undoubtedly are, they have their limits. The Adepts on our Earth are as yet relatively few in numbers, and are continually concerned with accomplishing the maximum of good by the exertion of a minimum of effort and expenditure of time and power.

Of course the Adepts could trace missing persons, but that would not generally be an economic use of Their power. In occult tradition, however, there are many stories of such ministration. We must remember that the occult life of those who come into close touch with the Adepts, and of the Adepts Themselves, is generally quite secret and never in any way advertised. The service is given, the work is done, and it does not matter who does it—that is the attitude in the occult life. Missing persons are constantly being found, apparently by purely human agency, but who knows whence came the first thought that turned the searcher, not only for people but also for truth, in the right direction? As far as our limited human mind can begin to grasp it, the chief work of the Adepts for mankind is to illumine the minds and exalt the Souls of human beings so that they won't get lost, whether in desert, bush or jungle, or amidst the perplexities of life. Surely it is far better to give one a chart of the course than to go about picking up strays? If the Adepts were to use Their time continually finding the strays of this world, They would be kept so busy that much of Their other and far-reaching work would be left undone.

What may we further assume that work to be? As I have just said, They perpetually flood the minds and Souls and hearts of human beings with inspiration, light, life, truth, with perception of principles and with courage and strength to overcome. In addition, age by age They find, preserve and give the truths of the Ancient Wisdom to the world. Such is part of Their great and major work for man, which is chiefly intellectual and spiritual. They tend to leave physical activities to human beings, whose work it rightly may be presumed to be.

Remember, also, that the work of the Great Ones is not limited to mankind alone. Their love, Their ministration and Their compassion embrace all that lives. " One of them [sparrows] shall not fall on the ground without your Father " (*Matt.* X: 29) said Jesus, and so Life in the mineral, the plant, the animal, the insect and the bird kingdoms of

Nature receives Divine aid. There, too, there is unfolding Life, ministration needs to be performed, and responsibility is accepted in the name of the Lord Most High, the Divine Source of all Life. Then there is the whole kingdom of the fairies and of the Angels, with its countless millions of beings, all of whom receive the ministration, the wisdom and the love of the Perfected Ones amongst men. It is this larger ministration for the whole Life Scheme, planetary and extra-planetary, which engages Their attention and effort, rather than intervention in the life of single human beings. Remember, however, that ministration to persons by Adepts is continually occurring, a notable example being the acceptance and training of men and women as disciples so that they, in their turn, may become servants of the Race.

Question: It seems a paradoxical situation to have a Fraternity of Adepts and Masters, capable of relieving suffering, when every year we read of millions of animals perishing of thirst in drought-stricken areas of the world.

Answer: I have already spoken of the necessity for the economy of power. We may be quite certain, however, that the restrictions and reservations of Adept aid are not so much on the part of the Adepts or the Lord Christ as on the part of man. Why do people suffer? Because of violations of the laws of Nature. This reaction to man's action is completely impersonal and very exact, even as is an injury from a fall caused by the operation of the law of gravity. Hurtfulness to another inevitably brings appropriate suffering to the one who hurts. Moreover, the extent of the pain is always exactly proportionate to the degree of cruelty. The Adepts have said that They often find Themselves helpless in the presence of the operation of this impersonal and exact law.

What is the best way to save people from suffering? Surely it is to tell them its causes, which are strong, coarse desires and the infliction of pain upon others. This the Great Teachers have continually done. "Love one another" has been Their gospel from time immemorial, as also has the fact of the existence and operation of the compensatory law. But humanity, like the people of Jerusalem in the time of Our Lord, will not heed. You will remember how Our Lord wept over the people of Jerusalem and said:

> "O Jerusalem, Jerusalem, thou that killest the prophets, and stonest them which are sent unto thee, how often would I have gathered thy children together, even as a hen gathereth her chickens under her wings, and ye would not!" (*Matt.* XXIII: 37).

Man's hardness of heart and inhumanity to man, as also to animals, remain proverbial.

The Adepts are relatively powerless in the face of humanity's heedlessness of Their teachings, and of human cruelty and its painful *kārmic* effects. Still They teach, both directly and through Their disciples and other agents. Still man will not heed, as every Buchenwald and every abattoir demonstrate. The Teachers continually tell the whole world to live in obedience to the law of love, and yet man will not obey that law.

Nevertheless, far more intervention occurs than is generally recognised. A wealth of testimony exists of spiritual, occult and physical assistance to man. Minds are illumined. Hearts are turned to the light. Bodies are healed. Human beings are visited spiritually, and even physically. No one ever cries for spiritual and intellectual light in vain. Yet all kingdoms of Nature must be aided. More helpers are therefore needed. Would it not be better to offer oneself as one who has tried genuinely to obey the laws of love and harmlessness and who is ready to help and to heal and to save, than to question critically the actions of Those who are the embodiments of love and whose whole lives have for countless millennia been spent in ministration?

Although the Adepts have attained to very great powers, even They cannot disregard Nature's laws. They know those laws so thoroughly that They can work with them perfectly, and so may *seem* on occasion to transcend them, but They never violate them. There is one law under which all happiness, all sorrow and all suffering comes, and even They cannot prevent its operation. It is the law of cause and effect and even Their strong hands, Their loving hearts, Their compassion, are often helpless in the presence of the operation of that law. The sufferings of men represent the retaliation of the law, which has been provoked by the infliction of sufferings upon others. As St. Paul said: "Whatsoever a man soweth, that shall he also reap." (*Gal.* VI: 7). Our Lord said: "And it is easier for heaven and earth to pass, than one tittle of the law to fail." (*Luke* XVI: 17).

So They, the Perfected Ones, seek to prevent our suffering by telling of the existence of the law, by teaching us to save ourselves by following the simple advice which They, age by age, have not ceased to give. In a phrase it is "love one another." Nevertheless, as I said before, a very great deal of such ministration and of healing from On High does occur in this world, and it is performed by none other than the Adepts and Their disciples. We should be just a little careful, therefore, before we criticize—though we may legitimately enquire—for we know so very little of what They do in service to the Race. Of this we may be sure; far worse, far heavier, would be the sufferings of the human Race were it not for this perpetual Adept ministration.

Do not let us forget that both the pleasure-giving and pain-producing effects of the operation of the law are highly educative. Unduly to modify or diminish either would not be beneficial. For example, the Principal of a University could, at the end of the year, look at the examination papers of a first-year student and say to him: "These are full of mistakes, but we will pretend that they are perfect and that you know the subjects thoroughly. We will pass you to a higher class." Would that be helpful? No, it would be neither helpful nor kind. Indeed, it would be a hindrance to the student's progress. There would be a serious gap in the student's knowledge and sooner or later mistakes would inevitably be made. Even as there were cities in which Our Lord did no mighty works because of the people's unbelief, so there are cases of ignorance, doubt, loss and suffering in which, taking the long view, it would not always be wise to use occult powers in order to give immediate, personal relief. I repeat, the law of cause and effect both ensures justice and is educative. Out of human experience wisdom is born. This, we may presume, is one of the reasons why in some cases the Adepts must withhold Their aid.

The Lord Buddha taught that ignorance and the suffering it causes can be dispelled by the knowledge of four Noble Truths. These are: the miseries of existence; their cause, which is ever-renewed desire for self-satisfaction; the destruction of that desire as the way of sorrow's ceasing; and the Noble Eightfold Path. This last consists of right belief, right thought, right speech, right action, right means of livelihood, right exertion, right recollection and right meditation. The Lord Buddha summed up this teaching in these words: To cease from sin, to attain to virtue and to purify the heart.

Economy of power, as previously stated, may be presumed to be one of the principles guiding Adept ministration to animals. Although I cannot here discuss the problem of animal *karma* and the various means employed by Adepts to help forward animal evolution, I am personally convinced that everything possible is being done by the Adepts for members of all the kingdoms of Nature on Earth. Furthermore, since man is the greatest enemy that animals have to fear, would it not be better to address questions concerning their sufferings to ourselves?

2. The Lord Buddha

Question: Is it a fact the Lord Gautama Buddha did not know he was the Buddha until He received the "illumination"?

Answer: As the question reads, if He was not yet actually and technically a Buddha, then, of course, He could not possibly have known that He *was* a Buddha. He must, however, have known at that time that He was a Buddha-to-be. Long, long ago the Spiritual Soul whom we know as the Prince Siddhartha, whose family name was Gautama of the Sakya clan, embarked upon that Pathway which leads swiftly to Buddhahood. In that last life on Earth His resolve came to fruition. First there had been born in Him the thought of Enlightenment in order to help humanity, which is the first step to Buddhahood; second, He had taken the vow to become a Buddha, and in the presence of One who had already attained to Buddhahood According to the immemorial rule, that existing Buddha had bowed, accepting the irrevocable resolve. So, before final illumination, the young man Siddhartha was a Buddha-to-be. He became a Buddha whilst seated under the *bodhi* tree on the night of the full moon of May, in His thirty-fifth year. Then, of course, He would know in full consciousness that He was Gautama, who had become a Buddha.

What, then, is a Buddha? "Buddha" is a technical term or title, not a name, descriptive of One who has reached a certain stage of enlightenment, has passed through the Eighth of the Great Initiations. The title comes from the *Sanskrit* root *budh*, meaning " wisdom "; so a Buddha is, in that sense, One who has attained to perfect wisdom, is Wisdom Incarnate, has reached the full summit of evolution attainable by man up to that time on this our Globe.

Question: Would the Lord Buddha before He attained supreme enlightenment just appear to the eyes of the world as merely a young man burning with a passion to "save the world" or, in other words, to find a solution to mankind's misery?

Answer: Yes, but not quite "just another young man". There is a spiritual light, a radiance, shining about such Beings, you know. Their Soul is awake and there is a strange fire burning within Them. They readily become inspired. As teachers, They draw men and women towards Them. They are sometimes great orators. So I do not think one so closely in that life approaching Discipleship, and especially Buddahood, would appear as just an ordinary young man. For many lives Gautama, the Buddha, will have been a remarkable Being, a lofty Initiate and Member of the Great White Brotherhood on Earth. These high attainments would almost certainly be evident in His physical appearance, even from boyhood.

Question: Most of the books concerning the Lord Buddha mention His "not-knowing" factor. Please comment.

Answer: Of course He knew that He was a Buddha-to-be. A statement to the contrary would be an exoteric blind. He was a full Initiate and Adept long before that last of all His human births. Read *The Light of Asia* by Sir Edwin Arnold and *Buddhism* by Christmas Humphreys, published in the Pelican Series, for further information on this point.

3. Spiritual Teachers and Their Teachings

Question: How should the statement attributed to Shri Krishna in the *Bhagavad Gita*: "He that neither loveth nor hateth is dear to Me . . ." be interpreted?

Answer: It is hardly for me to presume to interpret the teachings of so great a Being. However, since you ask me, I suggest that there are two possible interpretations. First, "He that neither loveth nor hateth—personally, possessively—is dear to Me." Secondly, I would suggest that Shri Krishna is referring to that equipoise between the pairs of opposites which He so strongly inculcated. This idea is like a golden thread that runs through the *Bhagavad Gita*. I would advise you to read both Dr. Besant's translation of that work and Sir Edwin Arnold's poem, *The Song Celestial*. The whole book is penetrated through and through with the call to attain to the equipoise of indifference to either heat or cold, pleasure or pain, love or hate, success or failure, each of which is to be regarded with just evaluation and equal composure. The message, I suggest, is the attainment of poise. Kipling was saturated with the idea, having lived in India. The poem *If* may have become somewhat hackneyed, but nevertheless it is a notable exposition of the ideal of such equanimity. Read the whole poem and note such remarkable lines as:

"If you can meet with Triumph and Disaster.
And treat those two imposters just the same."

Question: Where lies the difference between Theosophy and the teachings of Benedict Spinoza?

Answer: The difference is only one of scope, I think. Spinoza rather concentrated upon the Divine Immanence and ignored the Transcendence. Theosophy *is* partly pantheistic. It teaches of the all-pervading, indwelling presence of Spirit, the ensouling Life or deific Will-Force of the universe, but it *also* teaches of the Transcendent Logos. Some European philosophers delved into Hindu philosophy where the Ancient Wisdom, as Theosophy is sometimes called, is also to be found. They generally limited themselves to certain doctrines, so that their teachings have not the all-inclusive, all-embracing characteristic of Theosophy itself. Spinoza's philosophic system, which makes God the cause and substance of the universe and abolishes human free will, is not entirely in harmony with the teachings of Theosophy, though near to them. In Theosophy, man's spiritual will is not divorced from the Cosmic Will, but is regarded as an expression of it. In this sense man is thought to be possessed of free will. What the Cosmos wills, man in his spiritual essence, the Dweller in the Innermost, also wills and without the slightest sense of external compulsion.

PART FIVE

THE SPIRITUAL LIFE

1. The Spiritual Life Amidst Worldly Duties

Question: What is the meaning of a " dedicated life "?

Answer: A dedicated life would be an unselfish life, one utterly devoted to the service of God and the welfare of one's fellow men. That general definition can, however, be carried one step further. Individuals may decide that they could be more useful in the service of God and their fellow men if they were more evolved, more developed, greater in spiritual power. Then, in addition to service and worship, they will determinedly try to improve their character and increase their capacities, so that they may become more worthy instruments and expressions of the Divine Love and Life. They begin to live an inner life which hardly anyone else sees, striving to overcome their weaknesses, to develop the necessary powers, to gain realisation of the Divine Presence within and without them, of their unity with God and through Him with all that lives.

This deep, inner life is lived amidst all the outer activities. The life of service, which is visible, and the life of ardent aspiration, which is invisible, might together be called the "dedicated life". The truly dedicated persons have eliminated from their minds and their motives all thought of self, self-gain, reward and addition to their personal stature and prestige in the eyes of the world. Spiritually minded people have outgrown the desire for these gratifications, have emancipated themselves from the delusion that they are of any permanent value. If they seek power at all it is only in order to be more effective in what is called the Great Work, the fulfilment of the Divine Plan, and in service to their fellow men.

Question: If in this life one takes up the spiritual life, what can one do to ensure that the same opportunity is given in some future life?

Answer: If you take up the spiritual life—I mean the life of an active man and woman of the world who, illumined by spiritual ideals, tries to be Christlike in motive, thought, word and deed—then you will be doing almost all you can to ensure for yourself, under the law of cause and effect, a continuance of that mode of life in the next incarnation. Also, it is very probable that even better opportunities will present themselves in that life than have done so this time; for successful entry upon the way of the spiritual life is, like every other human experience, governed by the law of cause and effect.

One other step in that direction could also be taken; it is to adopt a regular regime of wisely ordered, daily meditation. This will tend to unify the consciousness of the Ego in its own world with the consciousness of the Ego in the brain. This achievement will be carried over into future lives, so that the Egoic determination to live spiritually in this life will be remembered and ratified in the next.

I would add that when the call to the spiritual life is felt, answer that call visibly and actually. Make a corresponding gesture of some kind, such as giving up an undesirable habit. Do this primarily for its own sake, but also because it will constitute a sowing of seeds from which there will be a reaping in terms of memory of the aspiration and also of conditions favourable to entry upon the spiritual life in the next incarnation. Whenever there is an inner spiritual experience, a true vision, it is important to recognise and ratify it physically by making some favourable change in one's character, one's habits and one's conduct of life. Then the way to further experiences remains open.

If, on the other hand, an inner call is disregarded and one goes on being much the same person as before, then the likelihood of receiving further inspiration could be diminished.

Question: Is the attainment of perfection easier today because we have great Teachers among us?

Answer: There are many men and women in the world today, leaders amongst men, some visible, some behind the scenes, helping on the progress of the Race, and it is true that as each one attains, the pathway is made a little easier for those of us who follow. Whenever you and I take one extra step ahead in evolution, we make it easier for all others—for all life is one. If a flash of illumination comes to us and we grasp a principle, that attainment thrills through the World-Mind and in some measure, however small, is shared by all. That is another ministration of the Great Teachers. By virtue of Their own self-illumination They illumine the minds of all mankind. So, yes, the presence of great minds, and of great men and women, does make the attainment of perfection easier. The Christ said: "I, if I be lifted up from the earth, will draw all men unto me." (*John* XII: 32). Similarly, progress for each individual becomes easier as the whole Race evolves; for the benefits of Egoic development are reciprocal.

2. The Path of Discipleship

Question: Would Mr. Hodson go a little further in his suggestion that we all offer ourselves as the helpers and assistants of the great Hierarchy. What does the Path of Discipleship mean? There are many people who are definitely on this Path of Discipleship. They have made a resolve that never will be broken, life after life, to lead a life of Discipleship. They still are one of us but they seem to have seen a goal—the Golden City of their dreams. I wonder if Mr. Hodson would say a little about this step.

Answer: Out of my very limited knowledge I can repeat what is to be found in our theosophical literature. I would recommend four books more especially to you. One is *In the Outer Court*, another *The Path of Discipleship*, and a third *Initiation, the Perfecting of Man*, all by Dr. Annie Besant. They are magnificent expositions of the subject. Those who wish to go still more deeply into it can hardly do better than read *The Masters and the Path* by C. W. Leadbeater. This is a very remarkable work, perhaps the most notable of its kind that has appeared in this century. I, myself, have contributed *Meditations on the Occult Life* and *The Pathway to Perfection.*

Yes, Theosophy does confirm the idea that the Path of Discipleship was not only open, found and trodden during the time of the ministry of Our Lord in Palestine. It has always been open and it will never be closed—never so long as there are those who aspire to find and tread it to its end, which is Adeptship.

Who are the true disciples of the great Teachers on our Earth? Well, they are men and women, young and old, who have had certain profound interior experiences. They have, for example, become aware of the sufferings and the sorrows of the world. They have also experienced so intimate a sense of unity with their fellows that they share those sufferings, are associated with those sorrows, almost as if they were their own. This awakens within them so great a compassion that they resolve that they will never rest ever any more until they have done their utmost to heal the wounds, silence the cries and soothe the tortured nerves of suffering souls, bringing peace to their hearts.

When that inner resolve, born of deep sympathy and a conviction of unity, is taken, a light flashes out and shines in the aura of the person. Then one or other of the great Adepts, it is said, to whose group that person belongs, one of the great Shepherds of Souls in whose flock that person is—and we are all in the flock of one of Them—observes the up-shining of the light in the darkness of the world's sorrow and selfishness, sees, as the mystical saying has it, that his or her " lamp is lit ". The Master then begins to flood that person with inspiration, to make opportunities and possibilities for them not only to serve more effectively, but to come into touch with Themselves. What almost appear to be accidents then bring the spiritually awakened person into contact with someone who has already attained Discipleship, and with groups of people who know about Discipleship, and thus a kind of gateway is opened. If they persevere they become part of some valid occult school and then sooner or later, it is said, they are drawn into the presence of one or other of the Earth's Adepts.

In Palestine this meeting occurred physically, as it has done in all the old civilisations and very much in India, and is said still to do in modern days; but for us in the West the meeting is generally superphysical, usually occurring in the hours of the night while the body is asleep. The Soul, the real, essential Self, is then freed and becomes drawn by the Master into His presence. In Him the aspirant finds One who embodies all the highest ideals of which he has ever dreamed. A Master of striking appearance is gazing upon him with eyes that see all and yet are filled with understanding and friendliness. The neophyte's superphysical senses are roused to the full, so that he knows perfectly where he is and what is happening, whilst far away, perhaps on another continent, the body is fast asleep. Then he is asked—either superphysically or physically, according to where the meeting occurs—whether, under his Master-to-be, he is prepared to dedicate his entire being, Spirit, Soul and body, to the most holy service of the Spiritual King of our Universe, the Solar Logos. All aspirants do not immediately accept the invitation, inconceivable though even hesitation would seem to be. You may remember, for instance, the passage in the Bible telling how the rich young ruler approached the Master in just this very way, physically in his case, asking: "What shall I do to inherit eternal life?" (*Luke* XVIII: 18).

First of all the general law is enunciated, partly as a preliminary test. "All these have I kept from my youth up" (*Luke* XVIII: 21), is the answer. Then comes the acid test, which is that of uttermost detachment and selflessness: "Sell all that thou hast,"—which is only a mental attitude, mark you—"and distribute unto the poor, and thou shalt have treasure in heaven: and come, follow me." (*Luke* XVIII: 22). He could not quite achieve that utter renunciation, as it seemed to him, though in reality it was only of a single rose for a tree that would bloom unto seventy times seven. And so "when the young man heard that saying, he went away sorrowful: for he had great possessions." (*Matt.* XIX: 22). In another life the chance would come again, or perhaps even later in that same life.

Others, of course, are so inwardly moved by the experience of meeting the Master that their head is immediately bowed in assent to His enquiry. They are then received into a kind of preliminary relationship officially called "Probation", blessed and shown certain desirable character changes, and work to be done. The link between the Innermost Self, the Monad, and the outer man is powerfully strengthened, so that the Aspirant may be increasingly self-inspired. This particular interview between Master and Pupil then closes. It may or may not be remembered on awakening, but certainly the flame of inspiration and aspiration to serve will be increased. Many such meetings will follow, until at last the official step of Acceptance by a Master is attained. Thereafter, especially while functioning in the superphysical bodies, that person is a fully conscious servant of the Communion of Saints, the August Assembly of Earth's Just Men Made Perfect. He has entered upon the life of Discipleship.

3. The Ancient Mysteries

Question: What were the "Mysteries of Initiation" practised by the First Century Gnostics, which preceded the " Mass " of Roman and Liberal Catholicism?

Answer: I would hardly be able to tell you, even if I knew. The very fact that they *are* the Mysteries of Initiation makes them profoundly secret, so that no Member of those Ancient Mysteries, not even a Candidate who had taken but the first Step, would say anything unduly revealing.

As for the Initiate who had reached that point where " Here ends all teaching. One sees Nature and all things ", as Clemens of Alexandria said, such an Initiate would never dare to reveal the Mysteries of Initiation under a penalty greater even than losing his knowledge and closing the Gateway to Initiation for lives to come.

I suggest, however, that the questioner studies the writings and teachings of the Gnostics, especially as collected in the books of G. R. S. Mead. Read also that wonderful book *The Secret Doctrine* by H. P. Blavatsky, and you will find therein much that was the secret esotericism of early days, but which now is being given fairly freely to the world. I do not know whether you realise it, but much for which I was a mere mouthpiece tonight in my lecture formed the secret teachings of the Eleusinian and Egyptian Mysteries, which were closely guarded and only revealed under the veils of allegory and dramatic ceremonial. It was secret in those days—hence much of the mythology and scriptural allegories of the ancient peoples—but as Theosophy it is now being verbally revealed, so that " he who runs may read ".

We need to remember, however, that the real esotericism can never be revealed by means of words spoken by one, however wise, to another, however eager. The esoteric, secret, Initiatory wisdom consists of interior experiences and the knowledge it bestows. Really *knowing* a thing means passing through it in your own consciousness and life, until it is yours for ever. So, whatever the revealed doctrines of the Ancient Mysteries were, the Initiatory secrets consisted, and still consist, of direct experience.

The main teachings included and still include, for the Mysteries are in operation today: knowledge of the nature, spiritual, metaphysical and physical, of both universe and man and their identity as Macrocosm and microcosm; the law of correspondences, revealing the relationship and interaction between the parts of the universe and the superphysical and physical bodies of man; the purpose of human existence and the means of its fulfilment, namely reincarnation; the law of cause and effect; dying and the life after death; the inhabitants of the superphysical worlds; the Directive Intelligence in Nature and Its embodiment in

Hierarchies of Angelic Beings, culminating in the Mighty Spirits Before the Throne and Their Synthesis, the Solar Logos; the science of collaborating with Them in the fulfilment of the great plan of evolution, "the Great Work"; magic, including thaumaturgy and theurgy; the Path of Swift Unfoldment; and the Hierophants and Adepts who have reached the summit of human evolution.

Remember, however, that these teachings, revealed as information in the Lesser Mysteries, become direct and continuing experiences in consciousness in the Greater Mysteries, through which Initiates pass Grade by Grade.

4. The Powers of Darkness

Question: Where do the Dark Forces come into the Great Plan? Were they created to provide needed opposition, or are they spontaneous destroyers, trying, for the sheer love of destruction, to throw spanners into the Divine Plan?

Answer: Dark beings arise in many ways. To the thrust of Spirit, which brings all Life to ever greater and greater fulness and beauty of self-expression, there is always resistance. "God's omnipotent power ever meets His impenetrable shield" it is said, and that resistance comes from matter. Whenever Life is embodied in a form, there is a constriction and a battle. This true, mystical Armageddon is being waged within us all, and to that resistance of matter there has been given a personified symbol, quite wrongly, of an embodiment of infamy and darkness, an isolated incarnation of evil—the Devil. He is only a personification of that resistance of matter.

In addition, certain men and women embark upon a way diametrically opposed to that chosen by the Forces of Light. Instead of wishing to become merged with the One Life, they seek isolation and separate power. Instead of seeking to help on the evolution of the world, they seek to divert, dispel and block it. Instead of being filled with love, they are filled with hate. They are all human beings and, unfortunately, there are many such in the world today, whether as world enslavers and dictators in international affairs, or as those who are deliberately gaining power and wealth through exploitation of the weaknesses of humanity—drug addiction, alcoholism, sensuality, for example. Slavery results, including a kind of economic slavery in which the people find themselves under heavier and heavier indebtedness to a small despotic group who constitute a financial oligarchy seeking to rule the world.

Yes, opposites of the great Lords of Light and Love do exist. They are the Lords of Darkness and hate. Each one of us has to make this choice and take our stand. Are we amongst those who are going to shed light and beauty upon the world, or will we, for example, plaster the cities of the world with ugly, sensuous hoardings in order to lure humanity into cinemas showing second or third rate films and to make money for ourselves? Those who use such methods of degrading others for their own gain become, consciously or unconsciously, agents of the Dark Powers.

* * * *

For the sake of readers of this book who did not hear the lectures which evoked such questions I give their substance, quoting from my book, *The Kingdom of the Gods*: [1]

" The existence of both Devil and evil is intimately associated with the attribute of free-will in man. Within the structure of cosmic law, and apart from the irresistible evolutionary thrust, man possesses the freedom to think, plan, speak and act either in accordance with Nature's purpose or against it. When, whether consciously or unconsciously, he operates against it, he becomes an antagonist of cosmic purpose. In consequence, he generates for himself adverse or ' evil ' experiences and conditions of life. If he continues, he tends to become cut off from the currents of the universal

[1] *Op. cit.*, Second Edition, pp. 170, 177, 178, 179.

Life-force, isolated, a being of death rather than of life. Some men have thus continued to exercise their freedom of action. They are the so-called black magicians, the Dark Powers, the followers of the Left Hand Path, the Lords of the Dark Face, the dread Brothers of the Shadow. Their destiny is not to be annihilated, but to sink into the condition known as *Avichi*, the ' wave-less ', the opposite pole to Nirvana to which the Adepts of the Right Hand Path attain. Ultimately, in a later cycle of manifestation, those who become highly developed embodiments of self-separateness re-embark upon the involutionary and evolutionary journey. Satan himself, if regarded as an existent being, would seem to have exercised this freedom; for at some time he must have chosen a path of individualistic, self-separative motive and action. . . .

" . . . Satan as the personification and incarnation of pure evil has, in occult philosophy, no existence by himself. Evil is but the absence of good. It exists only for him or her who is made its victim. *Demon Deus inversus est.* The Devil is the shadow of himself which a man sees when he turns his back to the light. Nature is neither good nor evil, and manifestation follows only unchanging and impersonal law.

" The existence and human experience of the duality of spirit and matter, light and darkness, motion and inertia, expansion and contraction, cause man to think of these as good and evil respectively. If resistance provides a fulcrum, then it is regarded as good. If it frustrates—as by the all-too-familiar 'malice of the object'—or harms man, then it is evil in his eyes. . . .

" . . . So, apart from human values and human experience, evil as an actual creation does not exist. The origin of evil is in the mind of man. All things can appear as either evil or good, according to human experience and human use of them. Shakespeare echoed this teaching in his words: 'Nothing is either good or bad, but thinking made it so.' (*Hamlet*)."

PART SIX

THE SACRED LANGUAGE OF ALLEGORY AND SYMBOL

1. The Life of Christ Spiritually Interpreted

Question: If I may digress from your subject I would ask—was Jesus at His birth the Son of God Incarnate? If so, who was it took possession of His body the last three years of His life before His crucifixion?

Answer: So far as I understand a very abstruse and deeply metaphysical subject, we are all Sons of God Incarnate and Jesus was in that particular in no wise different from ourselves. The essential Divinity in Him is identical with that of all mankind. This is sometimes called " the Spark of the One Flame ", meaning a component of the Divine Flame which is God. The term " Scintilla of the Spiritual Sun " is also employed to describe the Monad of man, which is thus regarded somewhat as an electron in THAT which is the Spiritual

Being and Light behind the physical sun, the Solar Logos—in Christian terminology God. So we are all essential parts of God and in our spiritual nature inseparable from Him. We are His children, His sons, in the sense that the God-Nature or God-Presence in each one of us is a manifestation or Ray of His very Being. We do not possess this Ray as our own separate Soul. We share it, for it is the spiritual, animating Principle in all created things.

Thus, each and every one of us is a Son of God incarnate in a body here on Earth, just as was the Lord Jesus—the man who in his human individuality knew temptation, wept, thirsted and shrank from the cup of his suffering, but later courageously accepted it. We are all Divine, Spiritual Beings, Prodigal Sons in the symbolical sense, in that a portion of our Innermost, Spiritual Selves has come forth from the Father's home into the deepest depths of matter, and fain would eat of "the husks that the swine did eat." (*Luke* XV: 16). The Race itself has embarked upon the journey of return and some individuals have said metaphorically: "I will arise and go to my father." (*Luke* XV: 18). These have set their feet upon the Pathway of Swift Return, have passed through the "strait gate" (*Matt.* VII: 13) on to the "narrow way." (*Matt.* VII: 14). Ultimately we shall *all* return " home ", meaning to our Spiritual Source and Centre, and with our inherent Divine powers made fully manifest. So, in that sense the Divinity of Christ is the same as the Divinity of every man; for there cannot be in existence two different or separate Divinities.

What, then, happened at the incarnation of the Christ? What is the meaning of the twofold term " Jesus Christ " ? If we look back to the literature of the early Church and the early Christian Fathers, we will see an idea expressed there which answers our questions. The Gnostics, as they were called, those who knew truth (the *Gnosis*) direct, taught and believed that, as the questioner seemed to suggest, after the Baptism there were two individuals present. First, there was the highly developed, almost perfected Jesus, an evolving Son of God, nearing the goal of human endeavour—Christhood. At His Baptism a supernormal—not supernatural—visitation to our planet and to mankind occurred. In Hinduism this procedure is referred to by a *Sanskrit* word, *Avatāra*, meaning a descent or incarnation of Deity, especially of Vishnu, the Second Aspect of the Hindu Trinity or *Trimurti*, of which there are said to have been nine up to and including the Lord Buddha. The tenth *Avatāra* is referred to as *Kalki*, who will appear at the end of the Iron Age seated on a white horse, with a drawn sword, blazing like a comet, for the destruction of wickedness, the renovation of creation and the restoration of purity.

In Palestine 2,000 years ago such a Divine descent occurred in the Person of a glorious Being, the Spiritual Teacher of Angels and of Men, to whom might justly be given the name of "Christ" (the Initiated, the Anointed). This Being used the Inner Self and mortal bodies of the Initiate Jesus, blending His glorious consciousness with that of the pure young Hebrew Disciple. Thereafter for the next three years it was not merely the highly developed man Jesus, great though He was, but also a splendid Being who made Himself manifest, a wondrous Spiritual Personage who at the Baptism, as the Voice proclaimed, overshadowed and became one with Jesus for the three years or so of the ministry.

Question: If, as the Christian Church teaches, the death of Jesus on the Cross absolves us from all sin, why should we have to work out our salvation by repeated incarnations?

Answer: Here the student of Christianity is confronted by one of those pairs of opposing and mutually incompatible ideas between which there can be no reconciliation. They cannot both be true and each one of us must make up our own minds as to which of them we are going to believe.

Personally I find myself greatly drawn to the utterances of St. Paul, who said: "Christ in you, the hope of glory" (*Col.* I: 27), "... work out your own salvation with fear and trembling. For it is God which worketh in you" (*Phil.* II: 12, 13) and "... whatsoever a man soweth, that shall he also reap." (*Gal.* VI: 7). These teachings appeal to me far more than the idea that my salvation depends upon the fruits, the attainments and the agonising suffering of some other Being, however glorious. This, however, is only an expression of a personal opinion, every Theosophist being left free to judge for himself. I must confess that I cannot mentally endure the possibility that the indescribable torture of the Christ upon the Cross some 2,000 years ago was essential for the salvation of my Soul, atones for all my sins, and so sets at naught the otherwise universal law of cause and effect. I believe that I, myself, pay for my own mistakes. In fact, I would not wish anyone else to suffer for my sins.

Also, I cannot see how such vicarious atonement would be useful. The sorrows and sufferings of life which follow naturally upon transgressions are educative. They are self-created and the Ego, watching them in operation, is learning and acquiring wisdom and knowledge, especially not to fall into the same errors again. If the whole of this chain of causation, this concatenation of causes and effects, is going to be wiped out, how can there be any individual education from individual experience?

This does not mean, however, that either the doctrine of the Atonement or the atoning ministry of the Lord Christ are to be set aside. Not necessarily so. Let me suggest a possible spiritual significance of the Atonement.

Briefly, one of the experiences which is said to be entered into by all those men and women who reach perfected manhood, "the measure of the stature of the fulness of Christ" (*Eph.* IV: 13), is that of being consciously at one with the Divine Spirit and Presence in every man. The Christ knows Himself as spiritually united, metaphorically as a bridegroom, with the Spiritual Soul of every man. Our Lord is thus said to be consciously at one with the evolving Spiritual Self of each and every one of us. If we could look into our own inner nature, as also into the Inner Selves of all other human beings, we would discover there the Christ-Presence and the Christ-Power. We would find Him pouring out into us His perfected Life and Light. Mystics have achieved this and bear testimony to the fact. This outpouring quickens our evolution, brings nearer the day of our attainment, reduces the tendency to error, strengthens us to bear pain and enlightens us concerning the meaning of our sufferings. True, we shall still be obliged to submit to the operation of the law of cause and effect. We must continue to reap, both pleasurably and painfully, as we have sown, but if we can respond to this enhancement of our spiritual power then our inner attitude, the way in which we receive both pleasure and pain, is spiritualised by this perpetual ministration of Our Lord. In what is really an at-one-ment rather than a vicarious atonement He, the Lord Christ, is sharing with us, not only for this present life but for all time, His own glorious, perfected Light and Life. It is not a transmission of blood and water down the centuries, but of perfected Light and Life which Our Lord in the at-one-ment continually bestows upon us all. There, I suggest, you have an acceptable concept of an atoning ministry, which still leaves room for both the educative effect of personal experience and the operation of the law of cause and effect.

Question: "Father, if thou be willing, remove this cup from me." (*Luke* XXII: 42). Could you throw more light on this?

Answer: This passage draws attention to one of the many problems confronting the student of the Gospel story. The problem is—and critics of the Bible draw attention to it—that in some passages the Lord Christ is portrayed as the Son of God, a mighty Cosmic Personage. He is identified by St. John with the Creator or Creative Power, the *Verbum*, the Logos, the " Word " by which all things were made. (*John* I: 1-5). He Himself said: " I and my Father are one " (*John* X: 30), " Before Abraham was, I am " (*John* VIII: 58), " I am Alpha and Omega, the first and the last." (*Rev.* I: II). Yet on other occasions, like the one here referred to, He displays human weaknesses—hunger, thirst, susceptibility to temptation, fears and shrinking from His task—just as an ordinary human being would shrink. This is contradictory and so poses a difficult problem.

Some scholars offer an explanation. They refer us to the writings of the early Church Fathers, particularly those known as the Gnostics, the " direct knowers of truth ". If you read their writings you will see that in the early Centuries of the Christian era they believed and taught that there were two beings—one human and one Divine—present in the person of Jesus the Christ; that their two lives became blended, and that all the humanities displayed by the Christ portray the experiences of a human being—Jesus—treading the pathway to perfection. The Christ-Presence, identified by St. John with the Creator, refers to another Being altogether, an overshadowing Power blended with the consciousness of the man Jesus as he trod his pathway through the five great portals of Initiation to the goal of perfection.

The Gnostic (*Vide The Gnostics and Their Remains*, King, pp. 100-1) answer to your question, then, is that it was the man Jesus who shrank from the sacrifice, not the Christ. It was the man Jesus who suffered, shed tears, experienced hunger and thirst and was crucified, whereas the Second Aspect of the Logos, the Cosmic Christ, had long ago transcended any such possibilities. If one is able to accept this old, traditional theory—and it is rather revolutionary, I admit—the problem of the combined Divinity and humanity of Christ is solved. There are modern Biblical scholars who lean towards this view that there are two stories in one—a manifestation on Earth of the Supreme Deity as the Lord Christ and also the trials of every Initiate—portrayed in the life and the experiences of Jesus of Nazareth. In the Apocryphal *Gospel of the Ebionites*, quoted by Epiphanius, it is stated: ". . . . they say Jesus was begotten of the seed of a man and was chosen . . . he was called the Son of God from the Christ that came into him from above. . ." Origen of Alexandria (Third Century A.D.), who was wholeheartedly identified with the early Christian Church, also taught the doctrine of the Incarnation of the Eternal Word or Cosmic Christ. This, he taught, required the mediation of a human soul and body, which were those of Jesus.

Question: Christ being perfect, why did He curse the poor old fig tree?

Answer: I appreciate your difficulty—and will suggest a way out of it—for indeed it seems un-Christlike to curse a fig tree, and still more so when we realise that the act was performed in the early Spring before the Passover, when in any case the fig tree could not have had any figs upon it; it was out of season. If read literally the story is contradictory, and even absurd. In that very absurdity, however, is said to be a clue. A learned Jewish Rabbi, Moses Maimonides, wrote in effect: "Every time you find in our books a tale, the reality of which seems impossible, a story which is repugnant to both reason and common sense, then be sure that the tale contains a profound allegory veiling a deeply mysterious truth; and the greater the absurdity of the letter, the deeper the wisdom of the spirit."

Here, then, is an incredibility which may spur us to look for the wisdom concealed beneath it. What could the message be? Remember that all the supposedly external incidents in the inspired Scriptures actually portray subjective experiences of man, interior changes and developments occurring as the Soul progresses from humanity to superhumanity. The message of this incident consists, I suggest, of the enunciation of a law—a profound law —that if we do not give forth of the "fruits" of our lives we shall wither away and die. He who seeks to have and to hold all for himself alone—particularly the "fruits" of his inner life, his discovered wisdom, truth and power—inevitably finds that his own inner and even outer life stagnate, inspiration leaves him, and eventually he withers away and dies. So attention is drawn to this great law—it might be called the law of flow—which is: give to live, share to enjoy, serve to unfold—the wondrous law of selfless giving in obedience to which alone life may be fulfilled.

It would seem, therefore, that it was not Christ who cruelly cursed the fig tree and caused it to wither away. The story is an allegory written in symbol, showing that he who will not give of the "fruits" of his own life and being, but keeps them hidden and hoarded unto himself—that person is as one dead, and sooner or later he withers away and dies as an effective human being. In addition to Our Lord showing this truth by His life, and teaching mankind to love one another, to give and to serve, both He and the Evangelists, as was the custom of the ancient teachers, also taught profound spiritual and occult truths in parable.

Question: What did Jesus Christ mean when He spoke of Eternal Life.

Answer: I must not presume to know what He meant. I cannot interpret His words in an authoritative sense, but I can offer a suggestion. There are two states of human consciousness, with an intermediary one linking them. One is time-ridden and cannot think outside of the familiar three divisions of past, present and future. That is the normal state of the human mind at present. There is, however, said to be attainable another higher state in which there is only an all-inclusive present, a kind of total here-ness and now-ness outside of the limitations of time, in which everything exists, as it were, in one place all at once and in fulness. The Deity is conceived of as existing in that state of consciousness, which is sometimes described as the Eternal Now. The attainment of Eternal Life may be regarded as realisation of this Divine state beyond the limitations of time, of space and of change.

For humanity there is evolution—whether physical, intellectual, spiritual or, as Theosophy teaches, all three combined—from the seed onward to the full flower in a succession of time. In the "eyes" of God, however, may it not be that the seed, the full flower and all the stages between exist and are perceptible at the same time? That is a state of full Cosmic consciousness. When that state is entered, Eternal Life is known. The Lord Christ may be presumed to abide in that state and to use the term "Eternal Life" in that sense.

The intermediary or linking state has been described as duration, or time without limits. Philosophers and mathematicians say that it is possible to pass from the limitations of past, present and future into a condition in which the present is enormously extended until, although there is still a sense of time, it is of time without limits. Whenever we become absorbed in an experience, particulary a happy one, we become unconscious of the passage of time. Nevertheless, Eternity is a mystery to us. One day we shall solve that mystery; then we shall enter into Eternal Life. Our Lord's words: "... he that hateth his life in this world shall keep it unto life eternal" (*John* XII: 25), suggest that one must deliberately withdraw one's selfish desires and exclusive interests from this physical world of time in order to enter a time-free state of consciousness—or to obtain Eternal Life.

Question: Will Jesus of Nazareth come to set up a personal reign on earth in future?

Answer: It would be quite impossible for me to answer that question in just this personal form concerning Jesus of Nazareth alone. If you would permit me to alter it slightly, making it rather more general, then I could say that there is a historical basis for the idea of the return of a great Teacher and Healer of Men. If you study the history of our time—and even pre-history—you will find a succession of cyclic appearances of great, wise, Godlike Personages, such as Hermes of the Egyptians; the Lord Vyasa, the Lord Buddha, Shri Krishna and Shri Shankaracharya in India; Zarathustra in Persia; then a little later Orpheus in Greece and, two thousand years ago, the Lord Christ in Palestine. Each of these Divine Personages struck the religious and the ethical key-note for the Nations which They visited, but if we study Their utterances we find Them both giving the same general teachings and promising that either They Themselves would return to earth or that They would be followed by a successor. The Lord Buddha, for example, definitely said that when He had gone another Buddha would arise, and that His name would be Maitreya—a word which means "Loving Kindness". So a great Lord of Compassion, or Loving Kindness, was promised to humanity by the Lord Buddha, to follow Him. Our Lord Himself said that under certain conditions, such as "wars and rumours of wars" (*Matt.* XXIV: 6), He would come again. (*Matt.* XVI: 27; *Luke* XXI: 27; *Acts* I: XI; *Hebrews* IX: 28). The Lord Shri Krishna said: "Whenever there is a decay of righteousness . . . and there is exaltation of unrighteousness, then I Myself come forth." (*The Bhagavad Gita*, IV: 7).

So, yes, there is some ground for a belief in the cyclic re-emergence of the great Teachers and Saviours of the Race, though it has not been Their practice to set up a purely personal, temporal, or even spiritual, reign upon earth.

The Hindu religion includes the idea of a succession of *Avatāras*, as They are called. The *Sanskrit* word, *Avatāra*, means "a descent", an incarnation of the Deity, especially of the Second Aspect, Vishnu. Unveiling would be a truer translation, for the Supreme Lord of the Universe cannot "descend" since He is also the all-pervasive Life in and by which we live. The Lord Shri Krishna is regarded as the eighth in the succession of planetary *Avatāras*. In some schools of thought—but not in Buddhism—the Lord Buddha is regarded as the ninth, and *Kalki* as the tenth, who is to appear at the end of the Iron Age symbolically seated on a white horse with drawn sword, blazing like a comet, for the restoration of purity. It is interesting to note that Shri Krishna also handed on His teaching work to the Lord Maitreya just before He passed away, saying: "For teaching the final [eternal] truths, thou art to approach reverentially Rishi Maitreya, son of Kushara [Kusarava]. When the Lord desired to leave this Earth, He gave this charge directly to Maitreya in my presence." (*The Bhāgavata Purāna*, III, 4, 26.

Quoted from *Theosophy in the Light of Hinduism.* Purnendu Narayan Sinha, p. 127).

2. The Symbolism of the Bible

Question: Could you please say something about the Feast of Corpus Christi as affecting this present Age?

(The lecture on Biblical Symbolism, after which this question was asked, was delivered on the Festival of Corpus Christi, to which reference had been made).

Answer: First of all I must dissociate the Theosophical Society from any one religion, and particularly from Catholicism. This Festival of Corpus Christi is celebrated in Christian lands, and generally follows Trinity Sunday. The words "Corpus Christi" mean the body of Christ, and the Festival of that name is held on a day set apart for a Celebration of the Holy Eucharist and the expression of gratitude to the Lord Christ for the provision of this Sacrament. Most Christians believe that a change occurs in the "substance" or existing spiritual content of the bread and the wine after the act of Consecration by a Priest, a measure of Christ's own Power and Presence being added. I would recommend to those interested a wonderful book upon the Sacraments of the Christian Church, written by the Rt. Rev. C. W. Leadbeater and called *The Science of the Sacraments*.

There is a text in the Bible in which Our Lord says: "Whoso eateth my flesh, and drinketh my blood, hath eternal life." (*John* VI: 54). Allegorists assert that these words, which admittedly could not be taken literally, were written in the language of symbol. The blood of God represents the ever-outpoured Life of God, the omnipresent, sustaining Life of the Second Aspect of the Blessed Trinity. Drinking that blood has been regarded as another symbol for interior realisation of the fact of the omnipresence of that Life everywhere, and of the identity of one's own Life with the Life of God. When the experience of identity with the Divine Life has been entered into, it is as if one were absorbing (as one absorbs a subject) God's omnipresent Life into one's consciousness and being. The act of drinking is a symbol for this experience.

Similarly, the eating of the flesh of Christ can only be taken allegorically, a literal reading being impossible. It is generally taken to be a symbol for full assimilation of Divine Truth, or the fundamental principles and laws of Life held in the Universal Mind or Third Aspect of the Blessed Trinity. The symbol for that Truth in the Sacred Language is the flesh of God or Christ, and the eating of that flesh describes in allegory the intellectual realisation of Divine Truth. When the Soul and the Spirit in us have realised, and thus " partaken " consciously, of the One Life of God in all and have absorbed the one Truth behind all, then we have emancipated ourselves from mortality and will enter into Eternal Life. From one point of view—the human—the text may be regarded as an allegory descriptive of realisation of unity with Divine Life and Divine Truth.

You ask how this will affect the Age. When a sufficient number of human beings have reached this stage of evolution, war will be outlawed and world peace will be established. The founding of Organisations to obtain international co-operation and unity foreshadows this achievement and its effects. Every one of us who by purity of life and daily meditation brings this attainment nearer, very greatly helps the evolution of the whole human Race.

Question: Does not the Bible say: " . . . it is appointed unto men once to die, but after this the judgment." (*Heb.* IX: 27)?

Answer: This question shows how unsatisfactory it is to quote from the Bible to produce final proof of the truth of anything, for one can find many utterances there which support quite opposite points of view. In one place the Bible states that " He that believeth and is baptized shall be saved;

but he that believeth not shall be damned" (*Mark* XVI: 16), and in another place you will find St. Paul saying: ". . . work out your own salvation with fear and trembling. For it is God which worketh in you . . ." (*Phil.* II: 12, 13). Both of these statements cannot be true; for one makes salvation dependent upon belief and baptism, and the other upon our own efforts.

So it is in the case of the quotation given by the questioner. Unless you give it a profound philosophical and not a physical meaning, it contradicts the theory of Reincarnation. That is admitted. I am afraid that I cannot offer you an interpretation under which such a statement as that can be true. If Reincarnation is true, then it is *not* given to man to die physically only once. His body dies over and over again; you and I have often died and been reborn and will continue to do so in the future. Our Lord Himself would seem to have affirmed this, for He said: ". . . Verily, verily, I say unto thee, Except a man be born again, he cannot see the kingdom of God" (*John* III: 3), and "Ye must be born again." (*John* III: 7). True, a kind of spiritual rebirth may have been implied, but this would not necessarily preclude the process of evolutionary ascent by means of successive lives on earth.

Question: Would you please explain the significance of Christ being crucified between two thieves, one on either side; also the true meaning of the words spoken to one of the thieves: " . . . Today shalt thou be with me in paradise." (*Luke* XXIII: 43)?

Answer: In suggesting an answer to this question, I wish to make it clear that I am in no way casting a doubt upon the historicity of the Bible, and particularly upon the accounts of the life of Our Lord. My suggestion (only) is that certain parts of the Bible—and I think this is one of them—are said to have been written in the Sacred Language, which is a language of allegories and symbols. In that language the thief is used as a symbol for the human mind; for the mind can be the great " robber " of intuitive perception and we are reading, remember, not of an external event alone, but also of an interior drama enacted in the life of *every* human being. The formal mind is symbolised by a thief because it can rob the Thinker of his realisation of unity with God, of knowledge of his Divine nature and of illumination by the activity of the intuition. The argumentative, concrete, scornful, acquisitive mind, the " lower " mind, is thus a robber, a thief, a " slayer of the Real ". This attribute of the human mind is personified by the scornful thief.

The Christ on the Cross personifies spiritual intuition shining through into the mind-brain. This light can only be received in the brain when the destructive, "thieving" attributes of the lower mind are separated from the more intuitive attributes of the abstract intelligence, personified by the other thief to whose words the questioner refers; for the mind is dual—higher and lower, abstract and concrete. One, the higher, is philosophic, intuitive, prophetic and synthesising, whilst the other, the lower, is concrete, factual, insists upon logic only, is limited to the present and the past and is analytical.

When the closing phases of human evolution are entered upon, as portrayed by the Crucifixion, these two become clearly separated one from the other and controlled. Symbolically they are "one on either side". Only when this is achieved can the full light of the Christ-Consciousness shine forth through the mind and the brain. The promise to the thief, who personifies the higher mind, "Today shalt thou be with me in paradise", is rather a recognition of the spiritual and immortal character of the true Thinker, the Ego in its vesture of light, which is its vehicle of abstract intelligence. This part of the mind goes onward with him to Adeptship or Ascension. The more analytical attributes, which can make man scornful of spirituality and intuitiveness, disintegrate at the death of the personality. Symbolically it does not enter Paradise or, in theosophical terms, Causal Consciousness.

The word " day " is used in the Sacred Language to describe an interior condition of spiritual illumination. Night, on the other hand, indicates mental blindness and an unillumined state of mind. Peter, for example, denied his Lord in the night, but was filled with remorse when day came and the cock crowed thrice. The word " today " in the passage quoted could therefore mean " at this time of spiritual illumination ".

Where did all this occur? At Golgotha, meaning " the place of the skull ". The skull encloses the brain-mind, which becomes illumined by the light of intuition, personified by the Christ, and the Initiate lives in a continuous realisation of unity with God. In placing the scene of the Crucifixion on the hypothetical Mount Golgotha, the inspired Evangelists, using the Sacred Language, underscored this particular interpretation of the great event. Such is one possible commentary upon the words of the Christ to which you refer.

Question: Would you please give us the meaning of the spear thrust in the side of Jesus on the Cross?

Answer: In one meaning the Crucifixion is really the spiritual coronation of the liberated or nearly liberated Initiate, who finally dies to self and self-separateness. The piercing of the skin, and therefore the thrust of the spear, in one sense means that the last faint " film " of the sense of separateness (the skin) is then pierced. Thereafter the truth of unity is known. Then it is that through the wounded hands, feet and body, blessing and power flowing through the open wounds can reach the world to sanctify and save it from far more serious and pain-producing transgressions than those into which otherwise it might fall.

The spear is also a symbol of the world's hate, which every Initiate of the Fourth Degree must voluntarily receive into himself or herself and transmute into love. There must be no self-protection any more. The heart is ever open to the world's evil, hatred, scorn and abuse. It must be so. It is the law. Part of the work of the High Initiates of our world is said to consist of that spiritual alchemy by means of which evil forces, interior and external, are transmuted into their opposites and sent out again as blessings upon the world. That action of willing acceptance and transmutation of evil demands a tremendous amount of self-control. The Christ-to-be must never wholly shut himself away from anyone, however ugly, evil, hateful or venomous they may be. To underscore this power of self-command, a symbol of discipline is used—a soldier drives in the spear.

If this is at all acceptable to you, you will have seen that mighty truths are to be found beneath the veils of the world's Scriptural allegories and symbols.

Question: Regarding the Parable of the Wise and the Foolish Virgins, according to Theosophy what happened to the five foolish virgins upon whom the door was shut?

Answer: I think the opening of the door—a symbol for an expansion of consciousness—is only a matter of time. No "door" is ever finally shut, nor can the processes of evolution be stopped. The Divine Will may be delayed of fulfilment, but it cannot be frustrated. There is an evolutionary epoch during which the seeds of spirituality, of intuitiveness and of the Christ-Consciousness, have not yet germinated within the human Soul. The foolish virgins personify the Soul in that condition. During that phase the Christ-Nature and the Christ-Power are not yet realised. In consequence, references to them make no impact upon the mind. Symbolically, there is no oil in the lamp. There does come a time, however, when the opposite is true, when spiritual awakening *has* occurred. That hidden, potent seed of spirituality and divinity which is within every one of us will one day germinate, grow and flower as the perfect man. Allegorically, all of us will one day find oil in our lamps and light them. The mind will then be ready and able to respond to the interior manifestations of the Christ-Nature in man and to be illumined by the light which comes from spiritual, intuitive perception. Symbolically, there *is* oil in the lamp, the wick is lighted and the coming of the Bridegroom —the Spirit-Self in man, the Logos of the Soul—is prepared for and recognised.

The human Race, it seems to me, is now showing signs of this spiritual awakening. The existence of great International Movements for the welfare of the world, such as the League of Nations, U.N., the International Red Cross, the Scout and Guide Movements and the Theosophical Society, indicates the awakening of the human mind to the fact of the unity of Life and the Brotherhood of Man. Symbolically, those members of the human Race who, like the foolish virgins, have been unprepared and unawakened spiritually, are now stirring in their sleep and beginning to dream of "the coming of the Bridegroom", meaning the attainment of the vision of the unity of all Life and its application in all human relationships. This awakening may be near to all of us. Ours to answer, especially when we begin to experience the preparatory "divine discontent", "the inexpressible longing of the Inner Man for the Infinite."

Question: Could you interpret Elijah's chariot of fire?

Answer: The chariot, as far as I understand it, is used in the Sacred Language in one sense as a symbol for the immortal vesture of the Soul which we call the Causal Body. The Gnostics called it "the Robe of Glory" and the Greeks "the *Augoiedes*", meaning "the self-radiant, divine fragment". At a certain stage in evolution, which is Adeptship, this "chariot" of the Monad becomes filled with a part of the fire of God and, thus enfired, the whole being of the Adept ascends in terms of consciousness, power and wisdom beyond the limits of the Earth and of mankind. The story is an allegory of liberation, entry into Nirvana, I suggest, rather than an account of a literal, physical fact, and the chariot may be regarded as a symbol for the Causal Body.

Question: What is the Outer Darkness?

Answer: A condition of self-isolation. It is not a locality, not somewhere to which the Soul goes after death or during life, but a state of being and of consciousness. Those who become excessively selfish isolate themselves from God, or rather destroy in themselves the power to realise the Presence of God, exiling themselves in the outer darkness of prideful self-separateness. Of course, even there—or even in that state, I ought to say—there is in reality neither absence of God nor darkness. It is only dark to those who are in that condition of consciousness. Actually, there is no place in the universe where God—and therefore light—is not, but some people become so utterly self-centred, self-motived, lost to the realisation of the truth of Oneness, that they cast themselves into what has been called " outer darkness ", a state of utter selfishness and of self-chosen separateness from all other beings. Their darkness is interior rather than external.

These people are the " spirits in prison " (1 *Peter* III : 19) to whom the Lord is said to have preached. The Ancient Mysteries teach that every human being who treads the " Way of the Cross " and passes symbolically through his or her Crucifixion on Golgotha, and death and burial in a rock tomb, must minister to the self-imprisoned ones in the outer darkness, or preach to the spirits in prison. There they try to rescue one or more, pointing out the folly of a way of life centred solely on self, and to awaken their minds once more to the desirability and the happiness of the way of light, which is the way of unity and universal love.

3. The Ancient Myths

Question: Please could you tell us of the symbol of the rose and the cross?

Answer: In its occult sense the rose is the symbol of the universal feminine, generative Principle. The rose is sometimes referred to as Nature herself, the ever prolific and virgin Earth, personified as

Isis, the Mother and nourisher of man, beast and plant. Thus the rose represents the femininity and fertility of Nature, also personified as Ceres, Venus and Ishtar. The rose was dedicated to Venus, Goddess of the generative energy in Nature. In this sense the rose (feminine) and the cross (masculine, though also dual) together symbolise universal generation.

The cross is not a symbol of death, but of Life—Creative Life made manifest. The vertical arm indicates descending Spirit, the positive, masculine potency of Deity, whilst the horizontal arm represents receptive matter, the negative, feminine potency of Deity. The intersection of the two arms, making the four-armed cross, portrays in symbol the active, creative process as a result of which universes are emanated and fashioned, or " born ".

In the microcosmic or human sense, when a man or woman has realised this dual Divine Presence and Power in themselves, the great secret that God and man are one is theirs in consciousness. They then know the inner meaning of the creative power and forces in Nature and in man, which is in part that the Deity of all is also present as the Indwelling, Creative Life-Force, Love and Will in every human individual. In the Rosicrucian Mysteries this interior experience of the Initiate was also symbolised by the rose and the cross. In the Egyptian Mysteries the Candidate was bound upon a cross, symbolising and foreshadowing conscious entry into this spiritual realisation. Sometimes the rose is pictured with its long stem twined round the lower part of the vertical arm. This suggests the serpentine path followed by the ascending, sublimated creative force in man—in *Sanskrit* called *Kundalini*—which elevates human consciousness into realisation of union with God.

The rose is guarded by thorns. So also, in the symbolical sense, is the Secret Wisdom which the rose also represents. Before the formal, lower mind can be fully illumined by the light of the abstract, higher Intelligence, a conflict occurs between the analytical, critical and self-separative tendencies on the one hand and the universal, synthesising, intuitively perceptive, selfless outlook of the Ego of man. In this interior battle, part of the Armageddon of the Soul, the " head "—the limited, formal mind or mental aspect of the personality—receives many " wounds". This mystical warfare is also indicated by the symbols of the rose, the cross and the crown of thorns upon the head of the dying (to self-separateness) Saviour. It is only to the populace, however, that the crown of the crucified Initiate looks like a crown of thorns. In reality it is a true spiritual crown, but the victory which it symbolises and the powers which it indicates evoke only scorn in the masses. To them it is a mockery, a crown of thorns. They cannot perceive what it *really* is and so they despise it.

The other symbol of royalty, the sceptre, also appears useless when it takes the form of a reed. To the multitude the reed sceptre is a mockery of royal power—whilst actually it is a symbol of spiritual power at its greatest, namely when exercised in gentleness. Thus, very deep mystical experiences concerning the crucifixion or death of the lower nature and the blossoming of the higher, like an open rose upon the cross, are portrayed by these great symbols. In the purely moral and ethical senses, the rose is the symbol of secrecy and the cross of self-sacrifice.

Question: Would you please interpret the myth of Persephone, which forms the subject of Lord Leighton's picture: "The Return of Persephone"?

Since readers of this book were not present at the lecture in which this myth was referred to, it is here briefly quoted from *Smaller Classical Dictionary*, Smith:

"Demētēr (called Ceres by the Romans), one of the great divinities of the Greeks, was regarded as the protectress of agriculture and of all the fruits of the earth. She was the daughter of Cronus and

Rhea, and sister of Zeus, by whom she became the mother of Persephone. Zeus, without the knowledge of Demeter, had promised Persephone to Aidoneus [Pluto]; and while the unsuspecting maiden was gathering flowers in the Nysian plain in Asia, the earth suddenly opened and she was carried off by Aidoneus. After wandering in search of her daughter, Demeter learnt from the Sun that it was Aidoneus who had carried her off. Thereupon she quitted Olympus in anger and dwelt upon earth among men, conferring blessings wherever she was kindly received, and severely punishing those who repulsed her. In this manner she came to Celeus, at Eleusis. As the goddess still continued angry, and did not allow the earth to produce any fruits, Zeus sent Hermes into the lower world to fetch back Persephone. Aidoneus consented, but gave Persephone part of a pomegranate to eat. Demeter returned to Olympus with her daughter, but as the latter had eaten in the lower world, she was obliged to spend one-third of the year with Aidoneus, continuing with her mother the remainder of the year. The earth now brought forth fruit again. This is the ancient legend as preserved in the Homeric hymn. In the Latin poets the scene of the rape is near Enna, in Sicily; and Ascalaphus, who had alone seen Persephone eat anything in the lower world, revealed the fact, and was in consequence turned into an owl by Demeter. The meaning of the legend is obvious: Persephone, who is carried off to the lower world, is the seed-corn, which remains concealed in the ground part of the year; Persephone, who returns to her mother, is the corn which rises from the ground, and nourishes men and animals."

Answer: The picture illustrates an incident in the Greek myth. The cave is both entrance to and exit from the Underworld or Hades. The God Hermes, with his Caduceus or Staff formed of a central rod and two intertwined serpents, is bearing Persephone from Hades below to the earth above. At the entrance to the cave is her Mother, Demeter, called Ceres by the Romans, into whose arms Hermes will deliver her daughter. Persephone, called Proserpina by the Romans, had been carried off by Pluto, King of Hades, and forced to become his Queen. Her mother, Demeter or Ceres, after long search discovered what had occurred, left Olympus in anger, lived on earth among men, conferred blessings when kindly received and punished those who repulsed her. At Eleusis she learnt the truth and appealed to Zeus, who sent Hermes to rescue Persephone. In consequence she was united with her Mother, as the picture shows. As, however, she had eaten part of a pomegranate in Hades, she was obliged to spend one third of the year there, continuing with her Mother for the remaining months.

This allegory has numerous meanings. In one interpretation Demeter is the Goddess of Nature and Agriculture, and Persephone is the seed, corn, plant life, or product of Nature, which sleeps below the ground during the four months of winter in the Northern Hemisphere. In Spring the resurgent, reproductive Life-Force—Persephone and Hermes together—brings forth and gives vitality to the new vegetation. This grows and its fruits ripen throughout the Summer, after which activity in the plant kingdom begins to die down, ceasing almost completely at the onset of Winter. Allegorically, Persephone again descends to the Underworld to become the enforced bride of Pluto, the King of Hades, personification of matter and the dark period of any cycle. Such is one possible interpretation of the story as an allegory of Nature's processes, in which Persephone represents the Life-Force in Nature, Hermes the power of reproduction and growth, Demeter the source of that Life and Zeus the Lord of the Universe.

A solar allegory is also unfolded, the time spent underground in Hades being the Wintertime in the Northern Hemisphere, when the sun lacks power for some three to four months of the year, thereafter rising to shine and give heat in the midst of the Heavens.

Applied to the Cosmos as a whole, the allegory tells of the Divine Consciousness which descends from its lofty spiritual state deeper and deeper into matter, until at last the deepest depths are reached —the mineral kingdom—symbolised by the Underworld. Then, in the course of evolution Spirit and consciousness begin to win free from the domination of matter, to shake off the shackles of materiality, and ultimately to become spiritualised. At the close of the cycle that which has been embodied and imprisoned is freed and returns to its source. Allegorically, Persephone is reunited with her Mother.

Cycles follow cycles and, as in the case of man, always in an ascending spiral. Persephone must therefore go down into the Underworld again and again. Recurrent cycles of generation and regeneration are also portrayed by other symbols, such as those of the serpent which regularly sloughs its skin, the scarab which rolls over and over the ball of mud in which it has enclosed its eggs, and the Phoenix which rises new-formed from the ashes of its body, which it deliberately burns every five hundred years.

In the microcosmic or human interpretation of the myth, Zeus personifies the Monad, Demeter the Ego, and Persephone the portion or " daughter " of the Ego which is incarnated in the body (Hades).

Before birth the Ego sends a ray or portion of its Life—Persephone—down from the Causal world, through the realms of mind and emotion (the upper air) into the physical world, to be born on earth (Hades) or married to Pluto, who personifies the elemental bodily desires. Every time a Soul is born to live in this darkened, material, physical body and world, Persephone, who personifies that Soul or ray of the Ego, has allegorically returned to the Underworld. In our purely human nature you and I are all as Persephones in Hades at the present moment. At death we shall be freed, eventually returning to the source from which we came, which is the Ego in the Causal Body (Demeter).

An occult interpretation of the myth is also possible. The Soul can prematurely win freedom from total imprisonment in the physical body if, symbolically, Hermes with his staff can be found to come and rescue it. The nature and structure of this staff give the key to the process of self-liberation; for in one interpretation, the human, the Caduceus represents very accurately the aroused serpentine, triple, creative power in man. When no more used for procreation, this power is transmuted or turned upwards until the two serpents' heads, or two oppositely polarised serpentine currents of creative fire, and the central rod or neutral current, enter the head. They then illumine and enfire the brain mind, thereby made responsive to superphysical powers and states of consciousness, or "freed" from the imprisoning limitations of the physical body. Hermes with his staff has, then, allegorically liberated Persephone from the Underworld. At the command of Zeus (the Monad) and with the submission of Pluto (the disciplined body elemental), Persephone (the personal Soul) is restored by Hermes (the Serpent Fire) to her Mother (the Ego in Causal Consciousness). From these human interpretations it will be seen that, as in the microcosmic meaning of every inspired allegory, the *dramatis personae* represent aspects of one individual, and the whole drama is enacted within man as an interior experience.

Such are some of the possible interpretations of this traditional story from the Eleusinian Mysteries, of which many of those who now find themselves deeply interested in Occult Science may have been members; for, in their outer garb, the Eleusinia were public spectacles and every distinguished citizen of Athens could become an Initiate of the Outer or Lesser Mysteries. At first they merely received and enacted the symbolic glyph. As they passed from the Outer or Lesser to the Inner or Greater Mysteries, allegory gave way to reality. Then, as the Initiating Hierophant touched the Candidate with the Wand or Rod of Power, the

Thyrsus, the interior, spinal forces symbolised by the Caduceus began to awaken. The Initiate was thereby freed from the body, which became entranced and was placed in the care of the Priests. The Initiated Soul, symbolised by Persephone freed, could then ascend into Egoic consciousness or become one with Demeter, its Goddess Mother.

The Caduceus has another meaning. That which I have already given is its possible dynamic significance, but it is also susceptible of philosophical interpretation, as are all the great symbols. The two serpents thus represent the pairs of opposites such as success and failure, heat and cold, pleasure and pain, happiness and despair, love and hate, health and disease, presence and absence, activity and inertia—all the opposites, in fact. Before the Soul can be perfected and fully liberated, it must have become equipoised in consciousness between all the pairs, being equally indifferent to either of their components. This attainment is called in Hindu philosophy *vairāgya* (desirelessness, detachment) and *upeksha*, another *Sanskrit* word meaning the poise of indifference, the dynamic balance between all pairs of opposites. This attainment implies that the whole nature has been brought into perfect equipoise, dynamic equilibrium, and has in consequence become relatively immovable, stable like the gyroscope. Then, as it were by the staff of Hermes, the Soul (Persephone) is no longer a prisoner of Pluto (bodily desires), is liberated, free. Such, in outline only, is a portion of the mystery of the Caduceus, such the story of Persephone, told only in the earliest of the Homeric Hymns.

Question: Would you please say a little about the symbolism of the Holy Grail?

Answer: The Cup, especially the Bowl, represents the vesture of light in which the Immortal Self of man abides, the Causal Body, the radiant vehicle of the Spiritual Soul of man. The Quest of the Grail portrays man's search for his own Divine nature. Actually, the Chalice represents the whole man. The foot is the physical body and consciousness, the aspiring emotions and the uplifted mind reaching towards the Cup or Bowl. This, in its turn, refers to the Causal Body and the higher mental, universalised consciousness of the threefold Self within it, to which the mortal man aspires. Wine is the symbol of spiritual wisdom, spiritual life, spiritual intuitiveness, the Christ-Nature in man. When successful, the questing mortal man, the Knight of the Holy Grail, " drinks " from the Cup. Once this interior Eucharist is enacted, the Christ-Consciousness is attained. The Quest of the Holy Grail has reached its consummation.

Each of the Knights in this immortal story is a personification of an attribute of man: Parsifal, the pure, unworldly, spiritually minded aspirant; Galahad, the utterly transmuted, depersonalised, selfless Soul—these two see the Grail. Lancelot, gallant, peerless, noble, but caught in the net of desire, sees not the Grail and, in one interpretation, ultimately brings to naught the King's rule, the reign of the Ego over the personality. Tennyson's *Idylls of the King* are replete with occultism. The colours and symbols are correctly conceived and applied. Tennyson must have been inspired though, of course, *Morte d'Arthur* by Mallory was his source of the great story. As far as is known, the romances first appeared in France and Germany in the Twelfth and Thirteenth Centuries, other countries deriving their forms of the legend from these sources. The Holy Grail legend whether in its Teutonic or Celtic form, emanates from the Mysteries and is another way of describing the quest for self-liberation, self-spiritualisation and the attainment of the Christ-Consciousness or, in a word, Initiate Knighthood.

PART SEVEN

THEOSOPHICAL ANSWERS TO HUMAN PROBLEMS

1. Ethical

Question: Do you think there is a ruthless band of "separatists" behind the modern money and banking system?

Answer: I must be careful in answering that question, because I must not involve the Theosophical Society, which is a living World Brotherhood, in any kind of a separatist opinion. The Theosophical Society does not take sides between man and man. If, therefore, a theosophical speaker makes adverse references to any particular person or group, he or she to some extent stains the white neutrality of the Movement. As that is one of its precious possessions, as an official representative of the Society I can only answer this question according to very general principles.

As an individual Theosophist, however, I can dissociate myself for a moment from the Movement and say that I fear that, indeed, just as there is on earth a Great White Brotherhood, whose members and co-workers accept and exemplify the unity of Life, so there is—I cannot say a band, because they won't even fully co-operate with each other—a number of human beings moved by diametrically opposite motives. They are isolationists, separatists, embodiments of selfishness, dark fanatics of the devilish creed of " self first ". These men are sometimes called by Theosophists the " Brothers of the Dark Face ". This is not because they act in a brotherly manner, but out of recognition of the fact that the Spiritual Essence within them is identical with that in all other beings. They are opponents of the Lords of Light, representatives in embodied form of the resistance of matter to Spirit and of the self-separative and acquisitive attributes of the human mind.

I fear there are such influences and people at enmity with humanity—not only in the great attempts at world enslavement by military force, the Police State, and in times of war, but continuously. I have been forced to conclude that an enslaving influence is constantly being exerted by determined, ruthless and intensely selfish people. A system of finance which perpetually increases human indebtedness to a few and demands interest on the ever-mounting debt, is one example of the activities of ruthless men with darkened minds, who are enemies of mankind.

Question: Would you discriminate between rugged, competitive individualism and rationalised, co-operative individualism?

Answer: Yes, I would, very sharply indeed. It is the utterly selfish, anti-social, ruthless, cut-throat competition—the basing of one's business life and enterprise upon the doctrine of " each for himself and the devil take the hindmost "—which surely is so wrong. This must, and one day will, be replaced by what you call " rationalised, co-operative individualism ", moving towards profit-sharing within businesses and the recognition of the right of all people to live and prosper. The thirst for life, the immoderate passion for possessions, the craving for riches and the physical power which riches can give—these are at the root of human sorrow.

A change is slowly occurring, however, and not only because it is found that profit-sharing can pay and that co-operative business enterprises can be very successful, but also because there is germinating in the human mind an idea which is pregnant with vast possibilities. That idea, that germ of a great truth which is now awakening in the human intellect, is the recognition that separateness is an illusion, unity the truth. Whenever we feel inwardly moved towards co-operation or, as it has been said, humanity experiences increasingly a hunger for wholeness, and as this hunger for wholeness and friendliness for each other grows amidst the spirit of competitiveness in life, then we shall have in the industrial, the business and the economic fields, and later in the whole world, a co-operative unity. Everyone who lives and earns co-operatively, even at some cost to themselves, helps to hasten the day of such a unified world order.

Competition is, however, a universal characteristic. Life in form must be persistent, reproduce itself, aggressively push out in all directions and successfully overcome obstacles or else risk elimination. In man this characteristic can become either accentuated to produce ruthless selfishness, or modified to the end of social adjustment and the elimination of competitive individualism. The aggressiveness thought to be necessary to provide security leads to intense competition in the individual, and this must eventually be controlled and redirected. Just as the cells of our bodies unite to form tissues and they in turn unite to form organs, each carefully separated from its neighbours but co-operating with them to form the human body, so society must find a way to combine separated functions and needs in recognition of the common goal of spiritual excellence and physical well-being for all. In the present phase of human evolution competition appears to be necessary to spur man on to his greatest efforts. Competition must therefore remain, but become civilised.

Question: Would you call the punishment of crime " cruelty "?

Answer: That depends, surely, upon the justice of the penalty and the method by which it is exacted. A dictionary definition of the word " cruelty " is " the infliction of unnecessary pain ". I must leave each one to decide for himself or herself whether pain suffered as penalty for crime is necessary or unnecessary. In the treatment of criminals I am myself drawn more and more to the two principles of segregation, as on penal farms, and of reclamation of character. Fortunately, as I think, the trend of penal reform in many countries is in these directions.

Capital punishment, one notices, is being no longer regarded by some Governments and people as justified, but rather as terribly cruel and, moreover, as not paying even lip service to reclamation. For myself—and not necessarily for the Theosophical Society—I would say that capital punishment comes under the heading of cruelty and will contribute *kārmically* to the adversities of those Nations which practise it. After some years of close study, my personal conviction concerning the distressing subject of the death penalty, whether by hanging, electrocution or the gas chamber, is that it is neither a deterrent nor a just sentence. In those countries where capital punishment has been abolished—there are about eighteen of them now and six States in the U.S.A. —there has not been an increase, but a decline, in the incidence of crimes of violence, particularly first degree murders. So the argument that capital punishment must be used because it is a deterrent to the crime of murder cannot be sustained. I therefore find myself forced to answer your question by replying that, for me, the punishment of crime by the death penalty *is* cruel. Murder *by* the State, I conclude, cannot be the best way to remove murder *from* the State.

Question: When we consider the redemptive nature of suffering, should we not welcome it on our own behalf as well as on behalf of others?

Answer: We may do as we like for ourselves, but should we not be careful about welcoming suffering for others? Whilst I recognise that, rightly received, one's own suffering can have a purifying effect upon oneself and thus be redemptive, I cannot believe either that pain is entirely essential to human progress or that it is ever possible to suffer seriously unless one has *oneself* previously generated that suffering under the operation of the law of cause and effect.

If one person so acts as to generate adversity, the reaction therefrom can with justice only come upon the original actor. If such a sequence of action and appropriate reaction constitutes immutable law, then some entirely different person cannot directly receive the reaction from the original actor's conduct. Neither could such a hypothetical recipient of undeserved suffering save the original actor from the results of his or her own actions and the educative advantages by which the operation of the law of such sowing and reaping is accompanied.

If the questioner should also be thinking of the redemption, or even helping, of others by voluntarily accepting undeserved, vicarious suffering—were such a thing possible—on their behalf, it is difficult to see how such acceptance of undeserved suffering could be very helpful to others. I doubt whether such a procedure would bestow benefits upon them which they could not better derive directly from their own experiences in life. I think a great deal can be learned vicariously by the wise observance and understanding of other people's efforts, failures, successes, happinesses and pains, but surely one does not need actually to go through the self-same or similar experiences either to help others or to educate oneself.

The law of cause and effect is at the heart of this problem. The Lord Buddha devoted some eighty years of His life to teaching people how to avoid suffering. Briefly stated, His teaching was that pain arises from craving; the cessation of pain depends upon the cessation of craving; the way to happiness is to kill out over-selfish and sensual desires and so avoid the pain-producing actions to which they lead. He summed up this part of His teaching in one statement: To cease from all evil actions, to acquire virtue, to generate all that is good, to cleanse one's heart and mind and to serve the world. This, surely, is a more reasonable way of freeing oneself from pain and of achieving self-education and spiritual progress than by redemption at the cost of suffering, whether one's own or another's.

Question: Do you think the rest of the world is likely to adopt the idea of Universal Brotherhood?

Answer: Certainly I do, if only because in due course the evolution of the human mind will bring it to a condition in which the unity of the Life in all men will be an observed and recognised fact in Nature. That direct, interior experience of the fact of Oneness will inevitably lead to brotherliness in motive, word and deed. Brotherhood does not have to be created, but only to be acknowledged, as it will be when the prophetic and intuitive aspects of the human intellect are sufficiently developed. A recent U.N. booklet indicates that this is occurring by its use of the expressive phrase: "No man is an island." (World Health Organisation Booklet).

We are, I believe, on the threshold of a new world epoch in which, as in all others, mankind will display typical mental characteristics. As I have said, those of the coming Age will be an intuitive perception of the unity of Life and its ratification as acknowledgment of the Brotherhood of Man. Therefore I answer: "Yes, definitely, world unity is bound to come." Even in the present Fifth Race, in which the analytical, formal mind is accentuated, this illumination is already being attained by many people. Hence the League of Nations, UNO with its specialised Agencies and all the other numerous Movements, including the Theosophical Society, based on world co-operation. You and I can help greatly by developing a vision of Oneness, by adopting and living up to the creed of kinship, by joining and working for the United Nations Association in our own city, and by being unifiers and harmonisers in our character and in our daily lives. By these means we can hasten the day in which this vision will be shared by the majority of men. Numbers count for very much in this development, and everyone who co-operates in all such ways quickens the historical process and hastens the dawning of the day of Brotherhood and Peace on Earth.

Question: Can psycho-analysis be included in the "helps" to eradicate faults of character?

Answer: As I understand it, that is not quite the purpose of psycho-analysis. Simply put, psycho-analysis is partly based upon the idea that our present mental, psychological and physical difficulties have their roots in forgotten or half-forgotten painful experiences, often of youth and childhood, and that if these can be brought back to the full, conscious memory and successfully eliminated, as it were, or resolved, then the trouble will disappear. That is the theory. Remove the hidden, and often forgotten, canker from the Soul or *psyche*, and the body will be healthy again.

You ask if psycho-analysis would be helpful in the eradication of faults of character. That would depend almost entirely, I suppose, upon the practitioner. A wise and intuitive psycho-analyst would doubtless be able to resolve complexes and so clear the way for positive action by oneself; for defects of character can only be replaced by their opposite virtues—the key to all such correction—by one's own positive efforts. An unskilful practitioner can do much harm, for it is one thing to awaken sleeping dogs—unpleasant or even shameful impressions remaining in the sub-conscious and suppressed by the conscious mind—and another thing to set them free. It is one thing to bring back the sorrows, the frustrations, the hidden griefs, the longings and the errors of childhood, and another thing to clear them completely out of the waking consciousness. It can be done and there are effective practitioners, but there are dangers inseparable from the procedure.

Do we really need anyone else to tell us our faults and help us to eradicate them? Surely we know most of them, if we have any capacity at all to see ourselves as others see us? Is it not less a question of our being able to observe our faults, than of being willing to recognise and acknowledge them? Some people resent reference to faults of character, even if they have asked for advice. They retire into a hurt moodiness, and even into a resentful gloom, eventually restoring their treasured self-esteem by affirming that they have been misunderstood. This self-delusion and self-comforting can be harmful, even though very natural and understandable. If we are really aiming to clear up faults of character, then we must be able and ready to see ourselves fairly clearly. Resentment, self-pity, self-excusing, have little place in the process of self-regeneration and character correction. Wise, external aid may be welcomed but, in the end, we ourselves have to do the work.

Question: It would seem that there is no room for self-pity in Theosophy. Unfortunate. But can we help and pity those who are oppressed by their own iron chains?

Answer: The whole ethical burden of the teaching which we have been studying together is self-forgetfulness, losing yourself in the service of others. Forget yourself in an ardent aspiration to bring about the welfare and the swifter progress of all, and in that very self-forgetfulness and self-giving in fulness and without reservation is found healing for oneself. Healing grace and compassion in life's difficulties then seem to flow into and through one, as one feels and expresses loving tenderness and pity for all. Self-forgetfulness is the basis of all happiness and all wisdom. So teaches Theosophy, as I understand it.

Theosophy is only a body of ideas and not a set of ethical commandments. Students of Theosophy can apply its teachings in any way they wish. It is not quite true, therefore, to say that there is no room in Theosophy for self-pity. I, myself, find that theosophical ideas encourage intelligent recognition of the causes of one's suffering. Since I realised that all suffering is self-produced and that its repetition can be prevented by wise conduct I, personally, have not found self-pity arising in my mind to any great extent.

2. National

Question: How could Iron Curtain countries best be told of our peaceful intentions, and their fears of a one-sided propaganda be allayed?

Answer: I do not know. That is work for world statesmen and at present it seems a fairly impossible task, if only because the truth about both their own rulers and those of the free world is deliberately kept away from the people behind the Iron Curtain. One method that is being used, as you know, is a continuous broadcasting, particularly by America and Britain, of propaganda in favour of the democratic way of life. These two countries have set up powerful broadcasting stations in Europe for this purpose. The present rulers of Russia try to "jam" them continuously, apparently being afraid lest truth should reach the masses. It is said that by means of broadcasts the Democracies are reaching an increasing number of people. That, perhaps, is one of the ways of making Allied intentions known, but remember that there can be no Iron Curtain against human thought, and especially against human love. If the world outside the Iron Curtain becomes increasingly full of true brotherliness, comradeship and friendliness, that volume of unifying influence will not only pierce, *but ultimately break down*, the Iron Curtain. That is where you and I can help, namely by broadcasting and living out in the world of our own lives unity, brotherliness, humaneness and the preservation of freedom for all mankind.[1]

Question: You have described a group of Nations which already exist practising co-operation with a bond of freedom. The British Commonwealth of Nations—is this not such a group?

Answer: Yes, amongst the number of unifications which have been achieved is that of the British Commonwealth of Nations; but, again, I do not want to give the impression that the Theosophical Society favours and thinks more highly of one group of Nations than of any other. That would be most untheosophical. Nor should an Englishman like myself, out of perhaps natural and proper pride, praise unduly the particular national group to which he belongs by birth. Nevertheless I think it may fairly be said that the British Commonwealth of Nations which, thanks to the Statute of Westminster, is an alliance of utterly free peoples, particularly as far as the Dominions are concerned, may justly be regarded as a kind of model for the future World Commonwealth which it is hoped will be brought into existence. Yes, the British Commonwealth of free Nations is to

[1] This question was asked and the answer given some time before the Geneva Conferences of Heads of the four countries in 1955.

some extent a reflection in the world of the "unreal"—meaning transitory, changing, evolving things—of that unity which forever exists in the world of the "Real", the world of Archetypal thought and eternal verities.

Question: Would not an international language like Esperanto be of great assistance towards world unification?

Answer: Yes, I think an international language would help greatly. Whether Esperanto will be the ultimate world language, however, I do not know. The tendency seems to be—and again this is not mere nationalism on my part—towards the adoption of the English language in many fields of world endeavour, including those of business and science, and one theosophical writer has suggested that this will be so for some centuries ahead.[1] The use of Italian for musical terms is one exception, though European nomenclature and signs in music are in world use. Whether the present so-called basic English will develop into a universal language, however, remains to be seen. Reports of Esperanto Congresses, especially those held on the continent of Europe, have been most enthusiastic. People who normally would have been separated by barriers of language could understand each other

[1] *Vide Man: Whence, How and Whither*, Annie Besant and C. W. Leadbeater, p. 457, 1913 Edition.

and the formal speeches straightaway, and this brought to the gatherings a wonderful sense of unity and brotherhood.

Question: Do you envisage a war between two idealogies—Communism versus Democracy—or a war between the different Races on Earth?

Answer: I cannot either don the mantle of a prophet or presume for one moment that I have more knowledge on this subject than anybody else. I have the theosophical key in my mind, however, and applying it, I believe that we are on the threshold of a new era and that a characteristic in the human mind of that Age will be recognition and ratification of the Brotherhood of Man. That, we are assured, will be the religion of the New Age —brotherhood, friendliness, " all-oneness ". I feel personally that the time is not far away when war will be unthinkable. I am sure that one day we shall look back with horror on the aggressive militarism of this period, just as we now look back with horror on the " Holy " Inquisition in Spain, Italy and elsewhere, the Concentration Camps such as those of Dachau, Buchenwald and Belsen, the reported slave labour camps in totalitarian countries and the brutal practices of the police states.

How soon world peace and humaneness may come about depends, I also believe, upon you and upon me. Our own private thinking and feeling are of immense importance, far more so than we realise. Just as a little trickling stream can wear away a dam or natural structure, until at last the whole is weakened and a great flood comes down, so the apparent trickle of your and my private hates and angers, malicious desires and irritabilities, can contribute towards great floods—or racial outbursts—of malice, hatred and passion; for there is a law of the conservation of energy in the inner as well as in the outer worlds, and all of this anger and malice in private minds and lives coalesces and makes a great concentration of anger, malice and desire to injure or destroy. Eventually some individual becomes a victim of and vehicle for this great force and commits a crime; some Nation then becomes an agent of humanity's cruel thoughts and desires. The "dams" of international custom and law then break down, releasing a flood of unbelievable ferocity and brutality.

The responsibility is not all with the single criminal or Nation which thus falls into error. Not one of us can truthfully separate ourselves from mutual responsibility for each other's actions. We one and all contribute to some extent to the criminal guilt of the world, great and small, individual and national. When you and I and the majority of men stop generating and giving expression to thoughts of discord, hatred, malice and disunity, and increasingly shed abroad the spirit of unity and love, then and not before will there be world peace. Whether a war with Nations now practising a grossly perverted form of Communism will be necessary before this can come about, I am unable to say; for the misdirection, the falsification and the degradation of the idea of equal sharing of both necessities and opportunities is militantly aggressive in the world today. The unfortunate fact is that a great deal of the same spirit exists and is also expressed in the so-called democratic countries. This gives an apparent justification for aggressive militarism and sanguinary revolution, and it also directly causes so much suffering and bitterness in its victims that they can be won over to the dark creeds of aggression and lawlessness. (See footnote, p. 93).

Question: How should one answer the statement often made: " There have to be wars to keep down world population, which would otherwise increase so much that there would not be enough food for all " ?

Answer: Wars temporarily reduce numbers, but they do not seem to keep down the world population. In spite of heavy casualties—some twenty millions in the first World War and forty-two millions in the second—the world population is now increasing by twenty-two millions a year. Whilst it is true that world food specialists warn us that we are facing a world food shortage, they also point to the cure which is, in a phrase, good husbandry. If we will only preserve the fertility of our soil we shall find that Mother Earth, thus husbanded, will give us enough food for all our needs.

The world's vegetarians have practical guidance to offer us in the solution of this problem. They say that the habit of passing plant foods through animals and then eating the animals is extremely wasteful. One-eighth alone of the plant food consumed by the animal is, it is said, received as edible flesh by man. There is a seven-eighths loss, because food animals are poor converters.

The mind is revolted—at least mine is—by the suggestion that more and more wars are necessary, and even desirable, in order to kill off the people and so keep down the population. The solution more probably lies in the discovery of new food sources, good husbandry and a less wasteful, plant food dietary. It has been proved possible to be perfectly healthy, mentally and physically, without the consumption of meat. The appearance since the War of World Humanitarian Societies, International Movements for the protection and welfare of animals, and recently an International Vegetarian

Union, indicates a growing recognition of these facts. This, surely, is the correct answer—and not a succession of brutal wars—to the problem of feeding an increasing population.

Aggressive war is a denial of love and can, therefore, only be regarded as evil. Entry upon war to prevent aggression is hardly in the same category, since it is waged sacrificially for the protection of the weak and the preservation of freedom. Arbitration is the enlightened way of solving difficulties between Nations. Good husbandry, a plant food dietary and the laboratory production of carbohydrates, fats and proteins by imitating the operations performed by the plant—these, surely, are the best ways of maintaining the supply of food for the increasing population of the world.

3. Religious

Question: Do you believe in God as a Personality?

Answer: What I believe is, of course, of far less significance than what is truth. What does Theosophy teach on the subject? Theosophy, as I understand it, does not teach of the existence of a personal God in the ordinary Christian sense. By that I mean a Being in human form, subject to the limitations of man, an angry, jealous God to be adored through fear and potent to destroy. Such, in part, is Jehovah, as portrayed in the Old Testament. I think that I could safely answer: "No, Theosophy does not include the idea of a supposedly Supreme Deity with purely human vices and weaknesses." Its teachings are, however, never uttered dogmatically, each Theosophist being free to form his or her own opinions.

There are at least two concepts of God, according to Theosophy. First, a Universal Triplicity of Will, Wisdom and Intelligence, operative as a Creative, Formative and Directive Principle throughout the Cosmos as a whole; or, to put it another way, God can be conceived of as the Creator, the Preserver and the Transformer of all beings and all things, and the Spiritual Parent of all men.

Second, to that idea is added a modification which makes the concept of our Divine Source and Father less remote. It is this. Our Solar System—the sun and the family of planets wheeling around it—is a unity within the whole Sidereal Scheme. Every star is similarly the sun or centre of a planetary family, and there are myriads of them. Over each there presides a manifestation of the Universal Deity, a distinct Individuality—though beyond the bounds of our imagination—for Whom the Solar System is, as it were, a body. This Individuality presides over it as its Power, Life, Intelligence, Law, Love, Beauty and Truth—an individual

Deity known as a Solar Logos, a Ray of Whose Presence shines in each one of us.

God, then, is not regarded theosophically as separate from man and far away in some Heaven. The Deity is within us all and is also the ensouling Power, Life and Consciousness of our little universe. So far as I understand it there are, as I have already said, two concepts of Deity contained in Theosophy—one is an abstract, universal, omnipresent, Divine Principle and Power from Which all things emanate, and the other is a manifestation of that Principle as the Deity of our Solar System, the Solar Logos.

Question: You referred in your lecture to a Solar Logos. Do you then infer that there is a separate Logos, or God-Head, for each separate star possessing planets?

Answer: Yes, definitely that is part of the undogmatically proffered theosophical teaching, though the term "separate" should never be applied to so lofty a Being, Who abides in fully conscious unity with the Life of the Cosmos as a whole. His particular Office, however, is performed within the restricted area of a Solar System, though His consciousness, and perhaps His other activities, doubtless range far beyond such a limitation.

Each star is a sun, a centre of planetary or other form of evolving Life. Over all there presides a mighty Intelligence, not a Ruler in the sense of a Dictator, but a Presiding Genius of Whom the whole System is an emanation and of which He is Architect, Engineer and Solar Emperor. Such, in part, is the theosophical teaching concerning the God-Head or Solar Logos as I understand it. I recommend for your study *The Solar System* by A. E. Powell.

Question: Did *all* Sparks come forth from the Logos at the very beginning of time, or is the Logos still emanating Sparks?

Answer: I must, of course, not presume to know very much about such lofty matters, particularly the processes which began to occur at the very dawn of the re-emergence of Life. As I understand the teachings, however, the emanation of Monads, or Divine Sparks, as they are sometimes called, and their projection of their Rays out into the evolutionary field, is gradual and continuous. All do not come forth and begin the pilgrimage of life at the same time. Those who are so far ahead of us now as to be virtually Gods, the high Adepts on our planet, for example, in most cases, though perhaps not in all, embarked upon the evolutionary process before we did. Actually, it is taught, the Monads are not emanated or externalised from their Source. They remain *within* It and project a ray of their power, life and consciousness into the evolutionary field.

Question: If God is the Spiritual Creator of all things, did He create the diabolical beings? If so, why?

Answer: To be technically correct, even at the risk of being pedantic, one would not use the word "Creator". "Emanator" would be better, for nothing is ever created out of nothing and the re-emergence of the Solar System and its components is only a rebirth of that which has existed before. One function of a Logos, it is taught, is to direct and preside over the emanation of a universe and to administer the laws thereof, laws to which even He Himself [masculine used for convenience only] is subject to some extent. One of those laws is that every human Soul must be left free. We human beings are not puppets dancing at the end of strings and created by Deity to be good or bad according to His Will. We are each Gods on our own account, if as yet but in embryo. In the use of our freedom, ignoring continuously given divine guidance, we can and do fall into selfishness and evil, and sometimes so deeply as to be classed as diabolical beings.

So, we cannot justly say that God created such diabolical, self-separated beings. Even if He could, He does not interfere with the essential freedom granted to all men, although that freedom may be temporarily misused to turn man into an evil creature. It is a strange and mysterious idea, is it not, that such followers of a self-chosen evil path—Lords of the Dark Face, Brothers of the Shadow, they are sometimes called (though, in reality, they are brothers to no one and have no brothers!)—can hinder the progress of evolution and, for a time, become or appear to become successful enemies of Deity? There is a sentence—a very striking one—which expresses that strange possibility: "God's omnipotent power ever meets His own impenetrable shield." I will not try to explain that saying—it is one of those thought-provoking utterances which one finds in the teachings of Theosophy concerning the relationship and interaction during periods of manifestation of the Spirit and the matter sides of Cosmos. (*Vide The Kingdom of the Gods*, Geoffrey Hodson, pp. 168-179).

Question: How is it that some apparently highly developed people deny the existence of God? Are they only greatly developed in their mental bodies?

Answer: Probably so, but this is an extremely important subject, if only because modern man might reasonably be said to be suffering on account of his over-accentuation of one aspect alone of his dual intellectual powers. The human mind is a two-edged weapon, a dual power. In its highest aspect and attributes it can conceive of the Divine. It can think of universals. It can conceive of unity as an underlying principle of the objective universe, with its appearance of diversity and separatedness. Indeed, the abstract mind *can* grasp the fundamental principles, equations and formulae behind related concrete facts and phenomena. It is also called the formless mind, whilst the other aspect of the human intellect is called the concrete, formal mind. The latter valuably analyses, criticises, argues, splits up, demands demonstration and ocular and logical proof. This, the concrete mind, *cannot* readily grasp fundamental principles, these being largely abstractions. It is, nevertheless, an extremely valuable tool for the Spiritual Self, but only as long as it is used for the right purposes. Amongst these are the discovery and examination of certain classes of ideas and facts; for until blended with the abstract mind, as I have said, it is not adapted to the grasp of abstractions and universals *and therefore tends to deny their existence.*

There are, as you have said, some apparently highly developed people who have concentrated upon the analytical mind, so that its development is greater than that of the rest of the thinking principle, causing it to overshadow the higher part of the mind. This is a rather dangerous condition to be in; for it can bring a person to that outer darkness, or monstrously accentuated sense of self-separatedness and personal pride, referred to in the answer to the last question and in Part VII, 1.

When excessively analytical, critical and separative, the formal mind will deny, shut out, inhibit the operation of that far higher intellectual power which is the intuition. The man who is limited to the use of the concrete mind tends to regard himself as a separated individuality whose own interests come first. The man who is able to use the abstract mind realises that "no man is an island". The higher mind and the intuition alone can reveal to the mortal man the fact of the universality and the unity of all Life. In radio terms, an over-developed formal intellect can "jam", interfere with, the receipt of signals from the higher aspects of the Soul; and so apparently great or mentally great men and women can come to deny the existence of a Deific Principle in Nature. True greatness lies in spirituality and in spiritual intuitiveness and wisdom.

I must, however, round this answer off with one further statement. What I have said is not a criticism of the power of what is sometimes called the legal mind, or of an approach to truth by its use. It has its very important place, and most especially for mystics, who are sometimes inclined to by-pass the reasoning mind. All ideas received in the higher states of consciousness must eventually be justified at the bar of the intellect.

There is an interesting episode recorded in the Bible which I think illustrates this necessity. It is the story of Doubting Thomas who, you will remember, insisted on proving things for himself, even to the apparent irreverence of touching the wounds on the body of his risen Lord, in order to assure himself of the Master's identity beyond all possibility of doubt. We may note that he was not rebuked. Rather was he encouraged, and when he had thus satisfied himself he exclaimed: " . . . my Lord and my God." (*John* XX: 28). By external test and proof Thomas thus found his way to his own interior light and certainty, but, be it noted, he did begin by a statement of his unreadiness to believe in the Resurrection until he received objective proof (*John* XX: 25). "Prove all things: hold fast that which is good", said St. Paul (1 *Thess.* V: 21); but, one might add, leave room for spiritual intuitiveness, that sudden flash of illumination which can reveal the soul and heart of all things.

Question: Is worded prayer more likely to be answered than thoughts, desires, actions and aspirations that are not expressed in words? In other words—does the former tend to wipe out *karma* associated with the latter?

Answer: May I suggest that you do not put these two—verbal and silent prayer—one against the other as if mutually prohibitive, for one can effectively use either or both methods. If to verbal prayer is added noble action, then the two together can produce miracles.

No, I do not consider that worded prayer tends to wipe out the *karma* of desires, actions and aspirations, as you put it. I think, however, that the Theosophist would say that prayers are less words to be said than aspirations and ideas to be meditated upon, and perhaps largely in the silence, the solitude and the sanctity of one's own heart. *There*, one can best commune with and contemplate God, ever seeking oneness with Him. When we have attained, in however small a measure, to this realisation of oneness, we shall have gained wisdom and strength with which to help the suffering world, and let us remember that service is itself a form of prayer. We can only become *karma-less* when the delusion of self-separateness has been completely outgrown and all actions are performed solely on behalf of the One Self of the Universe. This is the condition of the Adept who, in that sense, is said to be *karma-less.* Words cannot forcibly wipe out *karma* produced by actions. Only further compensating actions can do that.

4. General

Question: Can you please define the difference between the thinker and his thought?

Answer: The difference is much the same as that between the incandescent filament in an electric light bulb and the light that shines from it. One is the cause, the other the effect. The thinker is the Spiritual Ego which uses mind and brain, and his active use of them takes the form of human thought.

Question: Einstein states that the explosion of hydrogen bombs could make the atmosphere of the world so radio-active as to render life on this planet impossible. What has Theosophy to say about this—what of the Plan?

Answer: Theosophy is a group of ideas and can hardly be said to speak. If it did, I think Theosophy would first say: " Do not cross your bridges until you come to them ", and second, " the evolutionary plan is certain to be fulfilled." This I personally believe to be true. Humanity will *not* be wiped out from this Earth.

[The rest of the answer to this question was not given at the time, but thought out later on. I therefore replace the actual words recorded at the time with this later statement. The ideas were the same but their expression differed.]

Far from destroying humanity, the atom bomb may achieve what the United Nations has so far failed to achieve—the outlawing of war. Vast sums of money now spent on armaments could then be available for peaceful purposes and world tension would be relieved. How important these are! What an opportunity for human progress in every department of life would be provided by the abolition of war! This is not a mere idealistic dream. Any Nation which now embarks on war risks annihilation, and in the face of annihilation any Nation, or rather the leaders of any Nation, would pause. Thus we are on the threshold of a new era.

I say the leaders of the Nations, because the masses of humanity are longing for peace. They are experiencing what has been called a " hunger for wholeness ". Yet so far the terrible financial toll upon taxpayers for accelerated preparedness for war continues to be exacted. This has been admittedly forced upon mankind up to now. Adequate defences against threatened wanton aggression must be built up, as also effective resistance to it when it occurs. The certainty of disaster for both winners and losers in any future atomic war could, however, through fear bring about the abolition of war on Earth.

Thus the scientific discovery of the potentially annihilating atom, hydrogen and cobalt bombs may prove to be the greatest material blessing the world has known. Rightly used as deterrents they may lead to the abolition of war on Earth, to an era of peace and prosperity, and to a world civilisation founded upon recognition of the unity and solidarity of the human Race, the brotherhood of all men. This would also bring about the fulfilment of the First Object of the Theosophical Society, which is: To form a nucleus of the Universal Brotherhood of humanity, without distinction of race, creed, sex, caste or colour. It would be tragic if this came about only through fear. Idealists have seen a better way—the unifying of all humanity through love and understanding. This is the dream of Theosophists and it would seem that, despite the grave danger of the misuse of atomic energy, the world *is* moving steadily towards the fulfilment of the First Object of the Theosophical Society.

Question: When our Earth ceases to exist, how shall those who are in the mineral, plant and animal stages of evolution evolve further?

Answer: Briefly, this is not the only world, not the only planet, on which the evolution of Life is proceeding. On every star and on every globe in existence Life is unfolding at some level or other. It may be at the pre-mineral, or mineral stages, as evolution on some of the stars possibly is. Some globes may be at the mineral and plant stages only, or at the mineral, the plant, the animal and the human stages, as on our Earth at present. All planets are at differing levels of evolution, and when our Earth finishes this particular period of its life it will go to rest for a time and the Life Wave—the ensouling Principle and Monads of the mineral, the plant, the animal, the human, the Superhuman and the Angelic Kingdoms—will be swept on to the next planet which it will occupy, and will there continue its evolution from the level at which it left off here. This subject is more fully dealt with in a book called *The Solar System* by A. E. Powell.

PART EIGHT

MAN'S SUPERSENSORY POWERS

1. Psychic Faculties and Force Centres

Question: Does the occultist see the akashic record in its original form or does he see it in symbolic form?

Answer: In its original form. The trained seer, who has been properly taught by a Master of occultism will see the akashic record, or memory of Nature, correctly as it is. The half-trained and untrained psychic, who may still have wonderful powers, will always tend both to see or interpret incorrectly and to cast the results of inner experiences into some form of natural symbology. We are all inclined to do that with our dreams. Some of them are memories of experiences when out of the body, but as we wake up we sometimes cast them into a kind of drama, full of colours and symbols as of animals, reptiles, water, air, mountain tops or geometrical figures. It is this tendency which so often makes mysteries of our dreams and our visions. Each of us has our own system of symbology and, in general, we ourselves must learn to interpret our own interior and symbolised experiences.

Question: Has it ever been explained how the akashic records can be read without confusion, when so many millions of events are constantly occurring and must be more or less telescoped into each other?

Answer: I can only refer you to the radio. Concerts and programmes are filling the ether of the world, but as many of them are on different wave lengths they are not telescoped together and, for the most part, do not "jam" or interfere with each other. In consequence, our receivers can pick up a number of different programmes by tuning in on the appropriate wave lengths.

Whilst that is not a perfect analogy, it will help us to see how different events can be, as it were, available to a seer at the same time without interfering with each other. In reading the akashic records it is not so much a difference of wave length, however, as of time periods. The analogy of the scroll may perhaps be used; for when looking back into the past, the seer has the impression that the Centuries are moving before the mind's eye and he has the power to speed up or slow down the unrolling of the scroll at will. Of course, he does not really affect the akashic records at all. The change is only in his own consciousness as by his will he focuses, or tunes himself into, the time period he wants.

The usual method, apart from that employed by highly trained, Initiated Seers, is to take an object —if such can be made available— from the place and period which is to be examined. Let us suppose, for example, that something is brought from an old Egyptian tomb. Each object—a chip from a pyramid, an ornament from a mummy or whatever it may be—is pervaded and surrounded by a substance called the *ākāsha*, and upon that subtle, superphysical, spiritual essence there is imprinted the history of everything that has happened within its neighbourhood. If it be a stone the record will include its earliest deposit, the formation of the quarry, and the processes of its quarrying, its being carried to the building, the sweat and toil of the builders, and even the mind of the architect behind.

Once any portion of the akashic record is contacted it is possible, according to the powers of the seer, to branch out into the surroundings and see the civilisation of the time. He or she who does this begins by receiving certain mental pictures, as if on a screen in front of the head. The eyes generally close, the pictures appearing to the mind's eye as if in front of the forehead. As the student concentrates upon those pictures, his consciousness changes until he is no longer in the Twentieth Century looking back in time; he is transferred to the time and place concerned. His experience then becomes that of a spectator, but not only as a spectator. He can hear the sounds and even get a sense of the climatic conditions. He cannot, however, interfere in any way but can only watch, listen and observe. According to his powers, he can look backward or forward along a historical period.

An interesting aspect of this process is that in some cases it turns out that the seer had an incarnation, a life, in that civilisation. He may then be able to find that life and use his preceding personality as a focus from which to attune himself to the period, employ it as an outpost of consciousness, learn from it all that was in its mind, look out from it and so get a more detailed and intimate picture of the civilisation and time. It is partly in these ways that great seers have discovered that which for us is pre-history, and have checked and counter-checked their findings. An accurate record thus becomes available. Psychometry is one form of the power to read the akashic records.

Question: Is it not dangerous to try and pierce the veil?

Answer: If you would add the one word "unwisely", then I would say "Yes, it is dangerous to try *unwisely* to pierce the veil." Fortunately for us exact knowledge on the subject of the development of psychic powers is available and can be found in theosophical literature. The conditions and laws which may be applied to the safe development of the inner faculties are there described in detail. (*Vide Clairvoyance*, C. W. Leadbeater, and *Man's Supersensory and Spiritual Powers*, Geoffrey Hodson).

There are also certain laws governing the way of swift unfoldment, or the hastening of one's evolutionary progress, by the application of which the development of the supernormal senses can be brought about. Obedience to these laws enables a person safely to develop and use his psychic powers as instruments of research. The sort of person who would be advised to study, and perhaps practise, this science would be one who possessed the following attributes:

1. The motive is selfless—to know more in order to serve more effectively.
2. There are signs of a natural gift.
3. A great Teacher offers guidance.
4. The body is strong and healthy.
5. The emotions are controlled.
6. The mind is stable.
7. The physical circumstances both permit and point the way.

Motive is all-important. Theosophically, the only permissible motive for such endeavours is to become more effective as a servant of the Race.

Question: Is clairvoyant investigation of planetary life carried out by means of "the astral tube"? What is the astral tube?

Answer: I understand that occult investigation of life on other planets is generally carried out by means of a visit to them in the appropriate superphysical vesture of consciousness. This would probably be the Causal Body, from which level mental, astral and physical bodies could be materialised at will by a trained occultist. The astral tube would hardly be suitable for research for such great distances. The likelihood of interference would be too great and the energy required to prevent it would make a considerable drain upon the available supply. A high Adept would, I think, be able to be aware on other planets without leaving the physical body, though the latter would probably be almost entranced.

The astral—or rather the astro-etheric—tube is a projection from the pituitary gland, passing down the axis of the brow *chakram*, beyond the "petals" of which it extends an inch or so when not in use. It is portrayed by a serpent on the forehead of the Gods, Goddesses and Pharaohs of ancient Egypt. This serpent's head protruded from the *ureus* or serpent-like fillet of gold worn round the head. It also refers, however, to the serpent fire or *kundalini*, which must be roused and applied to the brow *chakram* in order to use the astro-etheric tube.

The outer end of this organ is projected towards the object to be studied. If the object is minute, then it can be enlarged almost indefinitely, partly by making the consciousness of the thinker correspondingly small, reducing it to the size of an atom, as it is said in Hindu occultism. If the object or place is far distant, then a kind of astro-etheric telescope or tube is used for investigation.

Question: To what extent can a healer influence a person suffering from an illness occasioned by *karma*?

Answer: *All* illness is occasioned by *karma*. Nothing can ever happen to anyone, or be set up in anyone, which they themselves have not caused. That is one of the great truths that every sufferer needs to learn and to accept. By accepting, I do not mean to surrender helplessly to it. Effort must still be made to overcome the difficulty. In the philosophical sense, however, and in the sense of this question, every illness is *kārmic*.

Perhaps behind this question there is another, such as whether spiritual healing would be an interference with *karma*? Would one, perhaps, be interfering with the working of the law in healing another? The answer to that, I understand, is that such a thing is impossible. No one, nothing in the universe, can interfere unjustly with a person's *karma*. It cannot be done, even by a hair's breadth, so universal, so exact, so unfailing, is the operation of the immutable law of cause and effect.

Then, too, the success or the failure of the healer's effort is also governed by *karma*. If the situation is very favourable, then even a small effort—a loving thought, a handshake and best wishes—can make a person wonderfully better, whereas in other cases one can pray and bless and seek to heal with an immensity of endeavour without result. True, the result partly depends upon the efficiency of the healer, but the *kārmic* situation of the sufferer is decisive. I have known sick people, after having been to various doctors and still remaining in great pain, begin to tell their story to some interested layman who has healing powers, and before they have finished they have discovered that the pain had all gone—nor did it return. What happened was that some inner tension and morbidity were removed by the confession and, the *kārmic* situation being favourable, interior healing forces were released and restoration of health occurred. Psychological tension is one of the great causes of psycho-somatic illnesses. *Karma* is, however, always involved. Even Our

Lord, you will remember, could not heal everybody. He did no mighty works in certain places because of the people's unbelief.

Thus, one cannot possibly interfere with another person's *karma*. If one's efforts reduce or banish their adversities that, too, is within their *karma*. Events recorded in the Press reveal the strange and selective operation of the law. A plane comes down in flames. Ten people are burnt to death. Three are injured and die after a few days. Two are unharmed and one becomes a hero and is rewarded, having saved others. A "blue baby" is born into conditions where there is poverty and no medical facilities for the necessary specialised operation, and so it dies. Another "blue baby" is born to parents with wealth and where the unique medical attention is available. It is operated upon and its life is saved. One can find an unfailing source of interest in noting the varieties of experience that befall people; for they are all explained theosophically as being due not to chance, but to the operation of the law of cause and effect.

Question: How can the Soul of a mentally defective person evolve?

Answer: Remember that the Soul is not mentally defective. If the questioner will allow me, may I say that this is an example of the way in which we in the West mistakenly identify the Soul with the body. The great Teachers have said: "Dissociate your inner Spiritual Self from your body and you will find peace. Identify yourself with your body and you will never find peace." In India, where these teachings are so well known, if not always followed, you may sometimes hear it said: "My body is hungry. My body is tired. I think I will take my body into the town." We, perhaps, need not go so far as that in words, but in thought we should. Then we would find much peace and serenity and also understand this particular problem.

The body and brain of a defective person are imperfect, perhaps injured, but the Ego within is whole. He is rather like a musical genius trying to play on a piano badly out of tune, or with missing notes, or without pedals, or with the pedals always down. In cases of mental deficiency, as also in cases of still-born children and children dying very young—which seems so purposeless—we should realise first that it is only the body which suffers and, second, that debts are being paid by the Spiritual Souls or reincarnating Egos, which are fully alive to the nature of such debts, are learning the lessons taught by experiences of reaction from preceding actions, and in consequence are growing wiser. In another life, the debt paid and the lesson learnt, the Ego will have a more perfect physical vehicle and use it more wisely than formerly.

Question: According to a book published in 1950, *The Mythology of the Soul*, the *chakras* are merely a form of mythology. Is this so, or not?

Answer: According to theosophical teaching, founded as it is upon the investigations of generations of seers, checked and counter-checked through the ages, these force-centres or *chakras* in the etheric, astral and mental bodies of man are a reality, and a very important one.

These whirling vortices in the normally invisible bodies of man are essential parts of the delicate and finely adjusted mechanism of consciousness, by means of which the Spiritual Self of Will, Wisdom and Abstract Intelligence is able to become expressed at the levels of the formal mind, the emotions and the physical world. They are no myth, therefore, but important realities. (*Vide The Chakras*, C. W. Leadbeater).

PART NINE

HEALTH AND DISEASE

1. Root Causes of Disease

Question: What would cause young children to have croup?

Answer: I can only give a general answer to enquiries about particular diseases, because there are many causes to be taken into consideration. Theosophy does not discount physical causes. Some diseases do have physical causes and some have mental ones, but there are generally predisposing factors in the *psyche* or mento-emotional nature of man. In the case of children these factors must have either been brought over from a preceding life or imposed in the present one by wrong treatment, or submission to continued emotional disturbance such as anger, irritation, excitability or bickering between the parents; for such influences are very contagious and children can be greatly affected by them.

In my lecture I touched very lightly upon the subject known to students of Theosophy as the law of correspondences. The inner Will of man, for example, is said to be represented in his body by the skeleton and its muscles. A bent or humped back, or other serious spinal complaint, may be the result of a misuse, to the injury of others, of the power of will or of the attributes of rule, lordship, pride. The saying, " A proud and stiff-necked people ", has within it more than a germ of the truth. Arthritis, for example, is found in many cases to occur in people of a very self-willed and prideful nature, and sometimes with rather rigid minds.

The emotional nature of man is in resonance with fluids. Even the common cold is sometimes more virulent, and may even have its onset, at times of acute emotional disturbance. The great influenza epidemic of 1918 struck the world at the most anxious time of the First World War, when the Germans broke through. I do not know whether or not this principle would apply to all children with croup, with its difficult and noisy respiration and hoarse cough, but this is the only contribution that I can make from a public platform and without a personal consultation.

2. The Theory and Practice of Spiritual Healing

Question: How might a person cure himself of an undesirable nervous habit which has lasted through many years, and has chiefly been indulged in when the mind is otherwise occupied?

Answer: I cannot prescribe for particular cases from the platform. It would be necessary to enquire very deeply into the sufferer's life, going right back to childhood—and even to pre-natal life—and so finding out when the symptoms first began and what happened at that time. Strains, trials, unhappinesses or shocks are almost certainly amongst the causes. For a complete cure it would be necessary thus to trace the habit back to its cause or causes to bring them to the surface of consciousness, and finally to free the subconscious and conscious minds of their influence. Then the re-education of the nervous system could begin.

In addition, the art of perfect relaxation should be learnt until it is possible to put the whole body, from head to foot, into a state of most perfect and harmonious equipoise, so that there are no habitually taut muscles or nerves. That requires a good deal of practice. When sitting in a car, for example, if one is not careful one mentally, and even physically, drives the car, puts the brake on, tenses up to oncoming situations, until this becomes a habit, often forced upon one through no fault of one's own.

Physical tension, perhaps, is at the back of this particular trouble, and therefore perfect relaxation could contribute to the cure. Watchfulness may still be necessary for a long time, checking the bodily habit, setting up a kind of mental sentinel which in time will automatically stop the undesirable movements—less by contraction and repression of the tendency than by bodily relaxation. However, skilled and possibly prolonged psychiatrical treatment and psychological readjustment by experienced and effective practitioners are often necessary to bring about complete cures of such deep-rooted difficulties.

Question: Is there any authentic case of an amputated limb being replaced by spiritual healing?

Answer: No, not to my knowledge. " Miracles " approaching that are recorded in the Scriptures of the world, but I do not remember having read of an actual replacement of an amputated limb in modern times.

The only case from the Christian Scriptures which occurs to me on the spur of the moment is that of Peter. In the Garden of Gethsemane, you will remember, he cut off the ear of the High Priest's servant, Malchus. Our Lord rebuked Peter, stretched out His hand, touched the place and restored the ear. (*Luke* XXII: 50, 51). Accounts also appear in the *Bhāgavata Purāna* of many similar " miracles " performed by the Lord Shri Krishna.

Question: How could I heal myself from emotional upset?

Answer: First of all, an effort should be made to reduce to a minimum the likelihood of recurrence of the physical causes of such troubles. Improve human relationships where possible. Then again, as I said in my lecture, take the opposite thought, namely—calm, poise, peace. Throw yourself into a mood of courage, poise, self-command. Resolve: "I will attain self-command, equipoise, this day." Give the order to the subconscious at night. Keep this up day by day, systematically, whether or not there is any result at first. The cure takes about three weeks as a rule. In this case of emotional disturbance, however, there may also be some root cause for undue susceptibility to emotional upsets, physical or psychological, in the experiences of childhood or youth, or when older. This also would have to be discovered, brought to the surface of the mind and neutralised or extirpated. Concentration upon the opposite quality, will to express the opposite power, determination to embody the opposite virtue—this process is a sure way of self-cure.

Question: Could you tell me the best method of eliminating fear caused through a psychic shock. The patient (a man) is most difficult.

Answer: In answering such a question, we have to remember that the solution lies in effective action rather than in a description of means. One can describe a method of healing verbally, with great detail, but unless the would-be healer has the gift or faculty of healing, the method will not work.

One way to overcome fear is to concentrate powerfully upon the opposite virtue, in this case courage, heroism, buoyant undefeatability. By this method one does not fight fear direct, though resisting its expression and over-riding its effects upon conduct as far as possible. Take a quarter of an hour two or three times daily, or less as time permits, and concentrate upon, contemplate, the remarkable quality of heroic courage. Think of some great examples of heroism like those typified by explorers and mountaineers—Captain Oates, for instance, Joan of Arc, and the winners of Victoria Crosses and other awards for courage. Think of yourself in that heroic guise until courage pervades you. Then, with all the will-power at your disposal, make a resolve that throughout that day courage shall be a characteristic of your thought and deed. Keep this up unwaveringly day by day until cured.

In this case, and in the case of the person with the nervous habit referred to by an earlier questioner, on going to sleep at night give an order to the subconscious mind—" I shall wake up in the morning perfectly relaxed and filled with courage."

Other positive attributes will be substituted according to the occasion and the need. Do not think of fear or of any negative characteristic. Do not say "I shall be fear-free", but "I shall be filled with heroic courage, dauntless, undefeatable." An Eastern Scripture tells us that "what a man thinks on he becomes". This is true and we can mould our character by constantly repeated thought. Indeed, this is largely the way in which character is formed. I recommend *Thought Power, Its Control and Culture* by A. Besant. (The above method is more fully expounded in my book, *Thus Have I Heard*).

Question: Please repeat the Healing Meditation you gave in your lecture.

Answer: Sit in privacy, relax the body, reverently but strongly turn the thoughts to the healing Source, visualising, for example, the Lord Christ with outstretched hands in His aspect of Healer. Then say with full intent: "May the healing power of the Lord Christ descend upon (Christian and surname), and may the Holy Angels encompass them. May the light of Christ's love enfold them for ever." (Pause, visualising the response clearly). "Amen." *Vide The Kingdom of the Gods*, Plates 23, 24 and 25 and relevant descriptions, pp. 235 and 236.

Sit quietly for another minute or so before going into the outer life once more.

THEOSOPHY AND THE THEOSOPHICAL SOCIETY

THE word *Theosophia*, derived from two Greek words meaning Divine Wisdom, was coined by the Neo-Platonists in the Second Century of the Christian era to connote the truths revealed to man by his Evolutionary Elders at the dawn of human life on this planet, and added to, checked and rechecked down to the present day by an unbroken succession of Adept [1] occult investigators. Theosophy, then, is offered to modern man as the accumulated Wisdom of the Ages, "an uninterrupted record, covering thousands of generations of Seers, whose respective experiences were made to test and verify the traditions, passed on orally by

[1] *Adept.* An Initiate of the 5th degree; a Master in the Science of Esoteric Philosophy; a perfected man; an exalted Being who has attained mastery over the human nature and possesses knowledge and power commensurate with lofty evolutionary stature. This fulfilment of human destiny is thus described by St. Paul: "Till we all come in the unity of the faith, and of the knowledge of the Son of God, unto a perfect man, unto the measure of the stature of the fulness of Christ." (*Eph.* IV: 13). Certain Adepts remain on earth to assist humanity and are referred to by St. Paul as "just men made perfect". (*Heb.* XII: 23). The Lord Christ similarly described the destiny of man in His words: "Ye therefore shall be perfect, as your heavenly Father is perfect." (*Matt.* V: 48 R.V.)

one early race to another, of the teachings of higher and exalted Beings, who watched over the childhood of Humanity . . . No vision of one Adept was accepted till it was checked and confirmed by the visions—so obtained as to stand as independent evidence—of other Adepts, and by centuries of experience." [1] The full fruits of this dual process have been preserved by the still-living Hierophants and Initiates of the Greater Mysteries, in which they were imparted to pledged neophytes alone. In their doctrinal aspect, these Mysteries consist of a vast body of teaching which embraces every conceivable subject to which the mind of man can be turned.

The fundamental principles of religion, philosophy, art, science and politics are all contained within this Wisdom of the Ages. From the time of the closing of the Neo-Platonic and Gnostic Schools to the last quarter of the Nineteenth Century, save for the few alchemists, Kabalists, Rosicrucians, occultly instructed Masons and Christian mystics, Theosophy was unknown in the Western world. Before then it was known and studied in various forms by the Platonists, the Pythagoreans, the Egyptians and the Chaldeans, whilst in India and China it has been preserved

[1] *The Secret Doctrine*, H. P. Blavatsky. Vol. I. 316. Adyar Edition.

down the ages in unbroken continuity. It is the wisdom of the *Upanishads* and the *Vedas*, the very heart of Hinduism, Taoism and Islam. By means of allegory and symbol it is revealed in the Christian Scriptures, the dead-letter reading of which has blinded Christians to their deeper significance.

The Theosophical Society, founded in New York in 1875, a reincarnation of innumerable similar movements in the past, is one of the many channels chosen from time to time by the Teachers of the Race for the transmission of this Ancient Wisdom to man. Theosophists are offered the opportunity of studying, living and presenting the age-old truths to the world in terms of modern thought. Though the presentations may vary, Theosophy itself, being all-Truth, is unchanging and eternal.

The study of comparative religion reveals the existence of certain doctrines which are common to all World Faiths. Although differently presented in each, when collected and blended into a whole these teachings constitute a basic body of revealed Truth which can be studied independently of all religious systems. Each world religion reveals an arc of the circle of Eternal Wisdom. Theosophy, although as yet but partially revealed to man, is the full circle of Truth. Age by age, at the direction of Those who are the Guardians of knowledge and its accompanying power, aspects of the Eternal

Wisdom are revealed to man through world religions and philosophies.

The great practical value of Theosophy consists in its revelation of the meaning and purpose of human existence, which without it is a hopeless puzzle defying solution. A puzzle may be solved by two methods. One is that of trial and error, of experimenting with various pieces in the hope that ultimately they will fit together. This is a slow and unsatisfactory method, particularly in the attempt to solve the problems of life. The other method, far more satisfactory, is based on pre-knowledge of the position of the various pieces in the complete design. Theosophy provides that knowledge, reveals the due place in an evolutionary plan of every individual and every event.

Life somewhat resembles a piece of tapestry. On the underside one sees little save incomprehensible tangles, knots, badly blended colours and a general confusion. Examination of the upper side, however, reveals the whole pattern, shows that the confusion is only apparent, since every juxtaposition is essential to the completion of the design. So, also, the apparent confusion in the lives of individuals and of Nations. Theosophy reveals the plan of life, thereby bestowing mental serenity upon those who study it and making intelligent and purposeful living possible for them.

The student of Theosophy will do well to recognise that the human mind, being finite, cannot fully comprehend abstract Truth which is infinite. As the human intellect develops, man's power of comprehension increases. Truth appears to change, as does the shape of a mountain gradually approached and seen from different points of view. The mountain itself is, however, relatively changeless, as also is eternal Truth. Theosophy being all-Truth, no final theosophical statement is ever possible. No theosophical teacher can legitimately make authoritative pronouncements. In the Theosophical Society opinion is therefore free, save, perhaps, concerning the brotherhood of man, which tends to be regarded as a fact in Nature to be recognised rather than as a dogma to be enforced. With this exception, no theosophical utterance is binding upon another and no statement is regarded as representing final Truth.

The Theosophical Society is officially described as being "composed of students, belonging to any religion in the world or to none, who are united by their approval of the Society's Objects, by their wish to remove religious antagonisms and to draw together men of goodwill whatsoever their religious opinions, and by their desire to study religious truths and to share the results of their studies with others. Their bond of union is not the profession of a common belief, but a common search and aspiration for Truth. They hold that Truth should be sought by study, by reflection, by purity of life, by devotion to high ideals, and they regard Truth as a prize to be striven for, not as a dogma to be imposed by authority. They consider that belief should be the result of individual study or intuition, and not its antecedent, and should rest on knowledge, not on assertion. They extend tolerance to all, even to the intolerant, not as a privilege they bestow but as a duty they perform, and they seek to remove ignorance, not to punish it. They see every religion as an expression of the Divine Wisdom and prefer its study to its condemnation, and its practice to proselytism. Peace is their watchword, as Truth is their aim.

"Theosophy is the body of truths which forms the basis of all religions, and which cannot be claimed as the exclusive possession of any. It offers a philosophy which renders life intelligible, and which demonstrates the justice and the love which guide its evolution. It puts death in its rightful place, as a recurring incident in an endless life, opening the gateway to a fuller and more radiant existence. It restores to the world the Science of the Spirit, teaching man to know the Spirit as himself and the mind and body as his servants. It illuminates the Scriptures and doctrines of religions by unveiling their hidden meanings, and thus justifying them at the bar of intelligence, as they are ever justified in the eyes of intuition."

On December 23rd, 1924, the General Council of the Theosophical Society passed the following Resolution affirming freedom of thought within the Society:

> "As the Theosophical Society has spread far and wide over the civilized world, and as members of all religions have become members of it without surrendering the special dogmas, teachings and beliefs of their respective faiths, it is thought desirable to emphasize the fact that there is no doctrine, no opinion, by whomsoever taught or held, that is in any way binding on any member of the Society, none which any member is not free to accept or reject. Approval of its three objects is the sole condition of membership. No teacher or writer, from H. P. Blavatsky downwards, has any authority to impose his teachings or opinions on members. Every member has an equal right to attach himself to any teacher or to any school of thought which he may choose, but has no right to force his choice on any other. Neither a candidate for any office, nor any voter, can be rendered ineligible to stand or to vote because of any opinion he may hold, or because of membership in any school of thought to which he may belong. Opinions or beliefs neither bestow privileges nor inflict penalties. The Members of the General Council earnestly request every member of the Theosophical Society to maintain, defend and act upon these fundamental principles of the Society, and also fearlessly to exercise his own right of liberty of thought and of expression thereof,

within the limits of courtesy and consideration for others."

Despite this complete absence of dogmatism, which should be the hallmark of all expositions of Theosophy, there does exist a general body of teaching, a synthesis of the common doctrines of world philosophies and religions, ancient and modern, which in practice is generally accepted *as long as it rings true.* Apart from the development and use of supersensory powers as a means of research, this constitutes a test which each student can apply to all theosophical teachings: *do they ring true?* If an affirmative answer is possible, they may be accepted as working hypotheses until fuller knowledge proves or disproves them. Should a statement not ring true, three courses are open to the student. He may reject, ignore, or suspend judgment until by self-training he develops the capacity to discover the facts for himself. The last of these three courses would appear to be the most desirable. Thus the attitude of mind in which Theosophy should be studied is that of the scientist—the acceptance of a well-supported theory as a working hypothesis until it is proved, disproved or suspended.

The writings of Madame H. P. Blavatsky constitute the primary sources of theosophical information in modern literature. Though branded as a charlatan by those who have neither investigated her life nor understood her literary work, this great lady is revered by tens of thousands of students of Theosophy as a light-bringer to the modern world. They believe her to have been chosen for this mission by the Sages [1] who have been both Guardians and Revealers of Theosophy to man throughout the ages. These Adepts used Madame Blavatsky as an amanuensis and with her aid gave Theosophy to the world in our time. Two main methods were employed. One consisted of fully conscious clairvoyance and mental telepathy in which, as a result of training under Them, she was highly skilled. The other method was that of the occult precipitation of letters written by Them, or by Their disciples at Their direction.

By the first method Madame Blavatsky produced her two great works, *Isis Unveiled* and *The Secret Doctrine*—each an almost inexhaustible fount of esoteric wisdom and knowledge. By the second method Mr. A. P. Sinnett, at that time (1880) editor of India's leading newspaper, *The Pioneer*, obtained the material for his books, *The Occult World*, *Esoteric Buddhism* and *The Growth of the Soul*. These authors have been followed by many others, notably Dr. A. Besant and Bishop C. W. Leadbeater, both of whom, in addition to the receipt of

[1] *Vide The Masters*, A. Besant.

direct instruction from the Sages, were trained by Them in the development of occult powers and their use as a means of research. Their subsequent contribution to human knowledge is immense.

The late Dr. G. S. Arundale and the late Mr. C. Jinarājadāsa, past Presidents, and Mr. N. Sri Ram, the fifth and present President of the Theosophical Society, all of whom are greatly respected theosophical leaders, teachers and authors, have also made their own valuable contributions. The late Mr. Jinarājadāsa collected and published many of the letters of the Sages to Mr. Sinnett and others, in three Volumes entitled *Letters of the Masters of the Wisdom*, Series I and II, and *The K. H. Letters to C. W. Leadbeater.* The interested reader is referred to these various sources as the bases for most of the statements made in this book. Since they are admittedly both general and incomplete, each of my main sentences should be prefaced by some such phrase as "According to my limited understanding". As this would be tedious, I ask that it be regarded as implicit throughout this theosophical study.

GEOFFREY HODSON

A METHOD OF MEDITATION

PREPARATION

Body relaxed.

Emotions harmonised.

Mind alert and charged with will.

Centre of awareness established in the Higher Self, the Spiritual Soul, the Immortal Ego.

DISSOCIATION

Mentally affirm and realise:

I am not the Physical Body.
I am the Spiritual Self.

I am not the Emotions.
I am the Spiritual Self.

I am not the Mind.
I am the Spiritual Self.

MEDITATION

I am the Divine Self. (Think of the Monad).

Immortal.

Eternal.

Radiant with Spiritual Light.

I am that Self of Light, that Self am I.

The Self in me, the *Ātma*,[1] is one with the Self in all, the *Paramātma*.[2]
I am that Self in all; that Self am I.
The *Ātma* and the *Paramātma* are one.
I am THAT. THAT am I.

CLOSING

Bring the centre of awareness:

Into the formal mind, illumined and responsive to the intuition.

Into the emotions, irradiated by Spiritual Light.

Into the body, empowered by Spiritual Will, inwardly vitalised, and Self-recollected throughout the day, remembering the Divine Presence in the heart, the Inner Ruler Immortal, seated in the hearts of all beings.

Relax the mind and permit the uplifting effect of the meditation to extend into the studies and the life of the day.

* * *

(For explanations and comments, *Vide A Yoga of Light*, Geoffrey Hodson, T.P.H., Adyar, Madras, India).

[1] *Ātma, Sk.* The Spirit-Essence of man.

[2] *Paramātma, Sk.* The Spirit-Essence of the universe, its presiding Intelligence, the Solar Logos, Our Lord the Sun.

BOOK LIST

The following titles are arranged in the order in which the books should be read to obtain, without undue digression, a progressive knowledge of Theosophy.

FOR STUDY:

An Outline of Theosophy	...	C. W. Leadbeater.
A Textbook of Theosophy	...	,,
First Principles of Theosophy and other Works	...	C. Jinarājadāsa.
The Ancient Wisdom	...	A. Besant.
The Great Plan	...	,,
Man, Visible and Invisible	...	C. W. Leadbeater.
Thought Forms	...	A. Besant and C. W. Leadbeater.
Thought Power, Its Control and Culture	...	A. Besant.
An Introduction to Yoga	...	,,
The Manuals of Theosophy, Nos. 1 to 7	...	A. Besant and C. W. Leadbeater.
Invisible Helpers	...	C. W. Leadbeater.
Esoteric Christianity	...	A. Besant.
The Christian Creed	...	C. W. Leadbeater.
The Inner Life, Vols. I and II.		,,

The Hidden Side of Things	...	C. W. Leadbeater.
The Masters	...	A. Besant.
The Inner Government of the World	...	,,
In the Outer Court	...	,,
The Path of Discipleship	...	,,
Initiation, the Perfecting of Man	...	,,
The Masters and The Path	...	C. W. Leadbeater.
The Light of Asia	...	Sir Edwin Arnold.
The Song Celestial	...	,,
Mount Everest	...	G. S. Arundale.
A Theosophist Looks at the World	...	N. Sri Ram.
The Human Interest	...	,,
An Approach to Reality	...	,,
Man: His Origins and Evolution	...	,,
Destiny	...	Geoffrey Hodson.
The Brotherhood of Angels and of Men	...	,, ,,
The Angelic Hosts	...	,, ,,
Reincarnation: Fact or Fallacy?	...	,, ,,
The Seven Human Temperaments	...	,, ,,
The Miracle of Birth	...	,, ,,
The Kingdom of the Gods	...	,, ,,
The Pathway to Perfection	...	,, ,,
Old Diary Leaves, Vols. I, II, III	...	H. S. Olcott.

REFERENCE BOOKS:

The Etheric Double	...	A. E. Powell	Indexed compilations which all serious students should possess.
The Astral Body	...	,,	
The Mental Body	...	,,	
The Causal Body	...	,,	
The Solar System	...	,,	
The Key to Theosophy	...	H. P. Blavatsky.	
Isis Unveiled	...	,,	
The Secret Doctrine	...	,,	
The Theosophical Glossary	...	,,	
Letters from the Masters of the Wisdom (Compilations)	...	C. Jinarājadāsa.	
The Mahatma Letters to A. P. Sinnett (Transcribed and Compiled)	...	A. T. Barker.	
The Science of the Sacraments	...	C. W. Leadbeater.	
The Hidden Side of Christian Festivals	...	,,	
The Chakras	...	,,	
Talks on the Path of Occultism	...	A. Besant and C. W. Leadbeater.	
The Lives of Alcyone	...	,,	
Man: Whence, How and Whither		,,	
The Story of Atlantis	...	Scott Elliott.	
Kundalini	...	G. S. Arundale.	
The Lotus Fire	...	,,	
The Science of Seership	...	Geoffrey Hodson.	
Some Experiments in Four-Dimensional Vision	...	,, ,,	

DEVOTIONAL BOOKS:

Christ and Buddha and all the smaller Books ...	C. Jinarājadāsa.
The K. H. Letters to C. W. Leadbeater and other Compilations ...	,,
The Practice of the Presence of God ...	Brother Lawrence.
Spiritual Maxims ...	,, ,,
At the Feet of the Master ...	J. Krishnamurti.
The Doctrine of the Heart ...	A. Besant.
The Bhagavad Gita (Translated)	,,
Viveka Chudamani (Translated)	M. Chatterji.
Light on the Path ...	M. Collins.
The Idyll of the White Lotus ...	,,
The Voice of the Silence ...	H. P. Blavatsky.
The Gospel of the Buddha ...	Paul Carus.
The Life of the Buddha ...	L. Adams Beck.
Thoughts for Aspirants ...	N. Sri Ram.
Meditation on the Occult Life ...	Geoffrey Hodson.
Be Ye Perfect ...	,, ,,
Thus Have I Heard ...	,, ,,
A Yoga of Light ...	,, ,,

OCCULT FICTION:

John Silence ...	Algernon Blackwood.
The Education of Uncle Paul ...	,, ,,
The Bright Messenger ...	,, ,,
The Centaur, and other Works	,, ,,
A Brother of the Shadow ...	Grace Colmore.

The Ninth Vibration	...	L. Adams Beck.
The Treasure of Ho	...	,,
The Garden of Vision	...	,,
The House of Fulfilment	...	,,
The Splendour of Asia, and other Works	...	,,
Om	...	Talbot Mundy.
Zanoni	...	B. Lytton.
The Coming Race	...	,,
Peter Ibbetson	..	Du Maurier.
The Perfume of Egypt	...	C. W. Leadbeater.
The Caves and Jungles of Hindostan	...	H. P. Blavatsky.
Karma	...	A. P. Sinnett.
The Youngest Disciple	...	Edward Thompson.

SPIRITUAL HEALING:

The Healing Light	...	Agnes Sanford.
Everyman's Search	...	Rebecca Beard.
Everyman's Goal	...	,, ,,
Everyman's Mission	...	,, ,,
A New Way to Pray	...	W. Mandleverer.
The Soul's Sincere Desire	...	Glenn Clark.
I Will Lift up Mine Eyes	...	,, ,,
How to Find Health Through Prayer		,, ,,
He Heals Today	...	Elsie Salmon.
Recovery	...	Starr Daily.
A Doctor Heals by Faith	...	Dr. Christopher Woodard.
A Doctor's Faith Holds Fast	...	,, ,,

Printed in the United States
977300001B